VOLUNTEERING

EMPOWERING YOU

The Rowman & Littlefield Empowering You series is aimed to help you, as a young adult, deal with important topics that you, your friends, or family might be facing. Whether you are looking for answers about certain illnesses, social issues, or personal problems, the books in this series provide you with the most up-to-date information. Throughout each book you will also find stories from other teenagers to provide personal perspectives on the subject.

VOLUNTEERING

Insights and Tips for Teenagers

JEAN RAWITT

ROWMAN & LITTLEFIELD
Lanham • Boulder • New York • London

Published by Rowman & Littlefield
An imprint of The Rowman & Littlefield Publishing Group, Inc.
4501 Forbes Boulevard, Suite 200, Lanham, Maryland 20706
www.rowman.com

6 Tinworth Street, London, SE11 5AL, United Kingdom

British Library Cataloguing in Publication Information Available

Library of Congress Cataloging-in-Publication Data

Names: Rawitt, Jean, 1952– author.
Title: Volunteering : insights and tips for teenagers / Jean Rawitt.
Description: Lanham : Rowman & Littlefield, 2020. | Series: Empowering you |
    Includes bibliographical references and index. | Audience: Ages 13–18. | Summary:
    "While many young adults want to help their community in some way, many are
    unsure of where to start. This book empowers teenagers to take action by providing
    information on how to get started, be successful, and make a difference. First-hand
    accounts from teenagers provide additional insight from those who have gone
    through the process themselves"—Provided by publisher.
Identifiers: LCCN 2020001458 (print) | LCCN 2020001459 (ebook) |
    ISBN 9781538129753 (paperback) | ISBN 9781538129760 (epub)
Subjects: LCSH: Voluntarism—Juvenile literature.
Classification: LCC HN49.V64 R39 2020 (print) | LCC HN49.V64 (ebook) |
    DDC 302/.14—dc23
LC record available at https://lccn.loc.gov/2020001458
LC ebook record available at https://lccn.loc.gov/2020001459

CONTENTS

YOU ARE NOT ALONE

Volunteer: A person who voluntarily undertakes
a service or duty.[1]

Volunteer: A person who works for an organization
without being paid.[2]

When I was fifteen, I was a volunteer "candy striper" (so-called after our uniform pink and white striped pinafores) at my local hospital. I learned a lot as a volunteer and have some wonderful memories from that time, such as how a woman who was blind taught me the "clock" method to describe to her what was on her dinner plate ("Your potatoes are at two o'clock, the sliced turkey is at six, and the carrots are at ten o'clock"). But I also remember things that scared me, like the fact that to get to the basement cafeteria on my break, I had to pass by an ominous door marked "Morgue."

Even so, the overall feeling that remained from that first experience was how *good* I felt as a volunteer; I loved the feeling that I was helping people, that when I walked into a hospital room with a smile, I was able to make a patient smile back. Even if I did nothing else, in that moment, I made someone feel better. That realization stayed with me for a long time—it's with me now—and it's the reason I've spent so much time in recent years volunteering, developing and supervising volunteer programs, and mentoring high school and adult volunteers during their volunteer experience. I want them to feel the same way I do—that whatever else I accomplish in my life, I *have* been able to help other people, cheer them up when they are feeling down, listen to them when they need someone to talk to, and assist them with things they are not able to do for themselves. When I wonder whether I am accomplishing everything I should be in life, when I am feeling overwhelmed by what I think I should be doing, I remind myself that, whatever else I do or have done, I *have* been able to make a positive difference to someone, some people, through volunteer service.

Volunteering is an important part of our nation's civic and community life, and it has been officially recognized as such. In 1974, President Richard Nixon first established National Volunteer Week with a presidential proclamation which included the following words:

> The spirit of voluntarism, one of the hallmarks of American life, has rarely been stronger than it is today. It has been estimated that one out of every five Americans is contributing time and talent in some kind of voluntary service. American volunteers are improving the quality of life in remote villages and in urban slums in the United States, and working to improve the quality of life for others in distant corners of the world. These efforts most frequently touch the lives of the poor, the young, the aged, and the sick, but in the process the lives of all men and women are made richer.[3]

But volunteering is certainly not just for adults: according to a survey conducted in 2005, an estimated 15.5 million youth—55 percent of youth ages twelve to eighteen—participate in volunteer activities.[4]

Volunteering can be part of an organized program, or it can be an informal offer to help someone that turns into an ongoing activity. It can be helping an elderly neighbor shovel snow or serving as a teen representative on a board of directors or community council. It can be teaching in a nursery school or offering to take photographs at a nursing home holiday party. It can be painting houses after a natural disaster or filling necessities baskets for parents of premature babies. It can be reading to people who are visually impaired or teaching skating to children with cerebral palsy. It can be an opportunity to work with people in your own community or a chance to travel to faraway places and work with people who don't speak your language or live very differently from you. It can be helping in a political campaign or playing music for disabled veterans.

In writing this book, I spoke to dozens of young volunteers and heard about the varied, valuable, and oftentimes creative ways they have offered their help in their communities, other parts of the United States, and other parts of the world. And what I heard from them most often was, "It just feels good to do good." I have also spoken with adults who work with young volunteers to learn what they expect from teen volunteers, what they look for in recruiting young adults for their programs, and how they train and supervise them. With this book, I hope to make it easier for young people to find ways to offer their time, skills, and hearts to help others.

The world is constantly changing, and so many of the changes seem to be negative—every day we are confronted with disturbing issues, whether it is direct exposure to hardship when seeing a homeless person on the street, watching news coverage of devastating natural disasters, or the horrifyingly violent acts humans perpetrate on one another. We see daily, whether online, or in life, how much is wrong with the world and how much suffering there is. And we may think—certainly, I do— how can I do something positive and productive to help fix the world and leave it better than I found it? And then I think of the things I can do with my free time—how there will always be people who need help and always be a myriad of ways to help them. And it gives me hope to know that while each one of us might dream of making the world a better place by doing something great, each one of us can, at the very least, do our part to heal the world by helping others in whatever way we can.

PART I

WHAT IS VOLUNTEERING?

CHAPTER ONE

WHY VOLUNTEER?

*The history of America is a history of volunteerism. Our people
have always worked together to resolve concerns, to fight injustice,
to rebuild communities, and to comfort those in need. And though some
regard today's society with cynicism and doubt, we need only look
to the more than 89.2 million volunteers who work tirelessly throughout
the year to see that we are still a people who care for one another
and who daily seek positive change by reaching out to others.*
—Bill Clinton, forty-second president of the United States[1]

As mentioned earlier, there is endless need in this world for people to help others. There are just not enough social services available to handle the immensity of the need, and so volunteers—people who step forward to help, out of the goodness of their heart, without pay, and often without thanks—help pick up the slack. Whether it is carrying groceries for an elderly neighbor, talking with a patient waiting to undergo surgery, painting a house for someone displaced by a natural disaster, or teaching English in an elementary school in a foreign country, volunteers take on responsibilities, offer comfort, and carry out tasks for no monetary gain, no personal recognition, and often no other reason than *it seems the right thing to do*. That is an enormously powerful motivator and perhaps the most important reason to be a volunteer.

There are, however, plenty of other reasons—which may not exclude the primary reason above—why you might become a volunteer.

If for no other reason, you might volunteer because it may seem like everyone you know is doing it. Depending on whom you ask and how you frame the question, there are different statistics as to how many young people are volunteers. Looking at the various studies, between 20 and 55 percent of young people do some volunteer work.[2] But there are many other reasons why you might become a volunteer. You might hear from someone you know about a volunteer activity in which they have participated and decide you want to volunteer as well. You might see a volunteer opportunity posted in your school or local newspaper, or on the internet, and decide it sounds like something you would like to do. Your school might have a community service requirement, for which you perform a certain number of hours of service to receive credit or qualify for graduation. You might develop an interest in helping people in your community. You might learn of a community devastated by a natural disaster and wish you could help in some way. You might decide it would "look good" on your college applications. Or, as many young people find, your parents might suggest (or push!) you to volunteer.

Whatever the reason you choose to volunteer, it is almost certain to be a meaningful and worthwhile experience—*if* you want to make it one. The valuable support young volunteers can provide takes many forms and offers the opportunity for a varied and worthwhile educational experience. A good volunteer experience will give you, the volunteer, as much or even more than you give to the people you serve. Being a volunteer can help give you a sense of purpose and value; it can give you a sense of responsibility; it can be an opportunity to make friends; it can teach you new skills; it can offer you a learning experience very different from what you might have in school or your usual environment; and being a volunteer can help give you a sense of confidence in your own ability to handle situations that are outside your everyday life. But for it to be a meaningful experience, you should be prepared to approach it with curiosity, openness, and a willingness to be of assistance to people.

Many young people find that there are often unexpected benefits to being a volunteer. One of the best of these is the chance to meet people whose backgrounds and experiences are different from yours and who you otherwise might not have an opportunity to get to know.

Evan C., a young musician, used to go regularly to a veterans' hospital rehabilitation unit to play music to the patients. "It was definitely eye-opening," he said,

> seeing people with missing limbs or mental issues. It was difficult seeing people who seemed pretty out of it. But I would play a lot of rock and roll, music from the 60s and 70s, the Beatles, that kind of thing. I would perform my set for about an hour. I was really nervous the first couple of times I did it, but then, after I did it a few times, I started to stay afterwards and I'd talk to the patients. We'd really develop relationships. I think being in the hospital must be pretty boring, and I think they enjoyed just talking with someone. One of the guys, I remember this so vividly, asked when my birthday was, because he was going use my birthday to play the lottery numbers. And they'd all ask for my autograph, which I thought was pretty funny. I have some great memories from that time. Talking to the people, seeing them perk up when I was playing, gave me a really good feeling.

The summer before high school, Evan had also signed up to work with an organization that helped senior citizens. He is not only a musician, but also very knowledgeable about technology, and one of the services the organization offered was to install simple computers with large monitors for homebound seniors so that they could connect to online classes or communicate with others at home. Evan was given the task of delivering the computers, setting them up, and teaching the seniors how to use them. He found that most of the seniors he was meeting were part of a large Asian community of mostly Chinese, Korean, and Vietnamese immigrants. "There were definitely language barriers," he said,

Evan C., a budding musician, volunteered to play for disabled vets.

and mostly I'd be trying to ask them what their password is or just moving their furniture around to get to the electrical outlets. But since I also had to teach them, there was also a lot of back and forth, like, "Do I do this, or do that?" But then they'd start to ask me questions about myself, and it was just so interesting to have these somewhat broken conversations with them. I even learned a little about their different cultures. I ended up having some really good talks, even without having very much of a common language.

On a recent family vacation, Shoshana had the chance to volunteer at a homeless shelter where her aunt works. She went to a meeting to learn about how to talk with the individuals at the shelter, what their lives were like, and what she as a volunteer should do. She was nervous about not being taken seriously because she was young and inexperienced as a volunteer, but she found that once she got there, she was treated equally. "The worry was the unknown," she says. "It's ok to be worried, not to know things." What she discovered was that she loved hearing the peoples' stories, learning about their lives, and trying to understand what they were going through. "It's important to get to know, to learn from, and to help people who are less fortunate. Volunteering opens your eyes," Shoshana continued. "Once you do it," she said, "You realize it's not only rewarding, it's fun. It was definitely a great experience. Most people should volunteer if they are able to. You'll see and learn about so many different people."

Being a volunteer can also give you a different perspective on your own life. Despite living in an affluent suburban town for years, Emily found herself surprised to learn that there were families living right near her own home who couldn't afford basic food supplies or drive their kids to school because they didn't have a car. As another young volunteer who worked with kids in a homeless shelter said,

Every time you volunteer you realize what you take for granted. When you see what others are going through, you start to appreciate that you know where your meals are going to be or that your parents don't have restraining orders against each other. Once, I was walking home from the homeless shelter where I worked as a volunteer and I realized that I was upset because my phone had a crack in it. And then it hit me—I'd just left people lining up for an hour to get a meal. It's very easy to get focused on such trivial things as your cell phone, but when you see people struggling with such hardships, it puts everything into perspective.

Cheyenne works with children who have physical and developmental disabilities in a therapeutic horseback riding program. Her first exposure to working with people with disabilities, Cheyenne finds it rewarding to be able to gain insight into their challenges. "Some of the riders are not able to communicate, but you see them start to come out of their shell when they are on the horses. They work so hard for the gains they make. It's a humbling experience," she said.

Some young people find themselves launching headlong into volunteer service when they become aware of a social service need. Emily, a teenager in New Jersey, found out for herself how difficult life was for some residents in her town. When she volunteered with her sister to put together gift baskets for new parents at her local hospital, she learned that the items on their wish lists were not toys or trendy clothes, but basic needs like socks, toilet paper, towels, and gift cards for groceries. She remembered thinking, if these items were on their Christmas lists, what do they need the rest of the year? Realizing that money was so tight for some people in her suburban community led her and her sister to launch a program to provide necessity baskets for new parents with limited means throughout the year.

The two teens worked together to approach local banks for funding to start their program, only to be turned away or advised to come back with a parent, or return when they were older. Undeterred, they worked for nine months to file the necessary paperwork with the Internal Revenue Service to qualify as a tax-exempt charitable organization, which they named "Project Hearts to Homes." Raising money; preparing the baskets; filling them with diapers, baby shampoo, and other necessities; and distributing them to hospitals takes an enormous amount of time

Emily and her sister started Project Hearts to Homes to fill laundry baskets for parents of premature babies.

and energy, Emily said, especially as her sister is now in college and the bulk of the work falls on her. On the other hand, she said, working with government officials, raising money, filing tax returns, and keeping up with schoolwork has forced her to hone her time management skills and certainly bolstered her communication abilities.

For some young people, volunteering can offer a chance to practice skills they hope to develop into a career. Jeremy, for instance, an avid photographer and videographer, volunteered to take photographs of his synagogue, which gave him a chance to explore techniques and develop his style, while giving the synagogue photos they can use on their website and in their newsletter. Marina hopes to pursue a career in medicine or related health services, and she said, "Volunteering in the hospital was a perfect fit!" Volunteering at the hospital allowed her to interact with patients and watch medical staff at work, and helped her develop her leadership skills when she was given the responsibility of acquainting new volunteers with the unit where she worked.

Sammy hopes to go into a broadcasting career. As a volunteer for her school's radio station, she practices her communication skills in her weekly announcements. As copresident of her school's United Way club, she also organized a basketball game as a fundraising project. Convincing the varsity players to devote a Friday night to having an unscheduled, out-of-season game took a lot of work, she found, but that, too, she said, helped her strengthen her communication skills—and confidence—when the game raised a record amount of money.

Volunteering can also turn out to be a gateway to an unexpected but rewarding career. As a young teen, Catherine fell in love with sign language. She had seen a book in the library illustrating basic finger language, and she practiced and memorized the images from the book. When she got to high school, she found that her school offered American Sign Language (ASL) as a fulfillment for the language requirement, and Catherine enrolled. At the time, she was also volunteering at a food pantry and one day noticed some people standing off to the side together and using sign language to communicate. One of the staff members who had gotten to know Catherine asked her to help them.

She'd only had three weeks of ASL classes but knew enough to help them, and she said, "I'll never forget how grateful those clients were, how patient they were with me."

During her senior year, she did an internship working with deaf children in a kindergarten class, interpreting for one little boy while he spent half a day in an integrated (nondeaf) classroom. These experiences solidified her appreciation for sign language and its culture, and she researched and chose a college that offered a degree in sign language interpretation. When she took one semester off and volunteered to work in a school as an interpreter for deaf students, she thrived in that role. After graduation, that same school hired her to work full time as a sign language interpreter, her dream job. "Get your feet in the door doing something you enjoy," Catherine advised.

> When I found sign language, I felt as though I fell down the rabbit hole—I was obsessed with signing. When I was a sophomore in high school, my parents couldn't believe how focused I was, that I was so sure I knew what I wanted to do. When I was volunteering, some of my friends couldn't understand why I was working for nothing, but I was paying my dues, getting experience, finding mentors, making friends, gaining knowledge. And it absolutely paid off for me.

One of the biggest advantages for young people of being a volunteer is having the opportunity to learn about different careers, change your mind about what you thought you would like to become, or broaden your existing interests. If you feel you already have a "passion," it's a wonderful way to delve deeper into it. If you don't yet feel you have one, volunteering is an excellent way to explore different areas and—possibly—develop one.

For a long time, Cheyenne has been interested in pursuing a career in medicine, but her work with kids with disabilities in a therapeutic horseback riding program sparked her interest in trying to incorporate health and wellness, and the physical and psychological aspects of medicine, into a future career. She finds that her volunteer experience has only reinforced and broadened her career goals.

As a volunteer, you may have a chance to meet someone who will become an important mentor in your life, helping you navigate educational or career choices even years after you first worked with them. These connections can be invaluable and even lead to lifelong relationships. When Catherine volunteered to work in a special ed class in a local elementary school, her supervisor really motivated and mentored her. "Where I was volunteering, there were a variety of students in the classroom, and some were very disabled," she said.

> I wasn't sure how I should be working with them and reached out to my supervisor. She gave me suggestions of how to teach them, how to build visual aids, how to communicate visually, and it really helped me. I stayed in touch with her over the years, and she was instrumental in helping me find a really rewarding job in that area. Staying in touch with her was one of the best things I could have done.

Throughout the years I have heard from many of the young people I mentored in the volunteer program I ran; some of them have kept in touch, keeping me informed on their academic progress or asking to meet me for career advice. I've written recommendations for jobs, scholarships, and medical school or other graduate programs, and it has certainly been gratifying for me to be able to help and hear how much their volunteer experiences have continued to have an impact on their lives.

Volunteers sometimes find that there are tangible rewards. One high school student was amazed to find at graduation that she had won an award for excellence in the "Service" category. Whether such recognition comes with a certificate, a special seal on your diploma or a trophy, or even a monetary award or scholarship, it can be a motivator to continue to volunteer. Such recognition and awards may even come from sources outside your school or community: there are corporate and even congressional awards for documented volunteer public service that carry significant prestige and honor for those who receive them.

Sometimes kids volunteer for things they perceive at the time to be great rewards. Jennifer, a young adult, now laughs when she talks about how her middle school had a mandatory community service program that culminated in an eighth-grade field trip to Washington, DC, with a group photograph taken on the steps of the Capitol. When she learned that the person who completed the most community service hours would get to be in the picture *twice*, standing at one end of the group as the camera panned the entire group and then running to stand on the other end and be included again, she was inspired to increase the number of service hours she worked to win what *she* thought was a wonderful reward. Looking back, she is amused by how childish her thirteen-year-old impulse seems, but she admitted that the early experience got her hooked on volunteering, and she has participated in many long-term volunteer projects since then.

Volunteers can also make a lasting impact on the lives of those they serve. Sometimes you learn immediately the mark you leave on someone's life—the gratification can be enormous when someone tells you, "I'm so glad you're here," or "You've helped take my mind off my pain." Sometimes the impact is unspoken but important nonetheless. Elizabeth's brother, who is on the autism spectrum, has volunteers who help him with various activities. For many people with autism, routine is important, and change and unfamiliar situations can be distressing. George looks forward to the volunteer who takes him for long walks twice a week and gets distressed if the volunteer cannot make it or there is a substitute. "He wants *that* person," said Elizabeth, "He wants *that* face, not just any face. The impact of human interaction on his life is so important, even when he cannot communicate why."

There are other practical reasons to volunteer. A recent survey showed that volunteerism can be an excellent pathway to employment, particularly for young adults sixteen and older who are at some risk—those who are neither in school nor working. Young people at risk who volunteered were shown to have a 5 percent increase in employment over similar youth who did not volunteer.[3]

If you still need more reasons to volunteer, here are two excellent ones: a recent study showed that on average, young people who volunteer do better in school than those who don't. And if that's not enough, the study pointed to the fact that young people who volunteer are happier—they scored 24 percent higher on a life satisfaction scale than those who don't. Not only that, but the more often young people volunteered, the happier they were. On a scale of one to one hundred, young people who volunteered once a week were more than ten points happier than those who volunteered only once a year.[4] So go for it!

CHAPTER TWO

GETTING STARTED
AS A VOLUNTEER

"We the People"—89 million of us—volunteer our time,
energy, talents, and material resources to create a better America.
There is no problem facing us today that volunteers are not addressing.
—Ronald Reagan, fortieth president of the United States[1]

People engage in volunteerism in many ways—as individuals, as part of a group, in their own communities, or abroad. At the end of this book you will find a list of selected resources where you can learn more about the many organizations that rely on volunteers. If you are going to find your own volunteer opportunity, that's a good place to start, and a later section will discuss things you need to know before you volunteer as an individual. The following are some other ways in which young people can give their time and energy to help other people.

FAMILY VOLUNTEERING

For many young people, their first exposure to volunteerism comes when they participate in a volunteer activity with their family. Very often it is a group activity organized through a community organization, place of worship, or school. Whether it is serving Thanksgiving dinner at a homeless shelter or preparing necessities kits for disaster relief, it is a

After seeing the destruction from Hurricane Sandy, Kate handed out supplies to those in need.

good way to start to see how meaningful it is to help others and how easy it is to do it. There are age-appropriate opportunities for every child and young person, and children are never too young to learn the pleasures of helping others. And parents who volunteer instill that inclination in their children. As a recent study showed, "Teenagers whose parents volunteered were significantly more likely to do so themselves."[2]

HOW A NATURAL DISASTER SPARKED A FAMILY'S RESPONSE: ONE YOUNG VOLUNTEER'S EXPERIENCE

A natural disaster—usually sudden and unexpected, and causing tremendous upheaval in dozens, hundreds, or even thousands of lives—can bring out the best and most spontaneous volunteer actions. Kate, now a freshman at Harvard, talked with me about how much impact it made on her, at age thirteen, to have seen the results of a natural disaster and been directly involved in helping the people most affected by it.

After Hurricane Sandy, the most destructive and deadliest storm of the season, whipped through the New York area in October 2012, it flooded entire neighborhoods and caused hundreds of people to lose their homes. Seeing early reports of the destruction and wanting to do something immediately helpful, Kate's parents headed to the local Costco and Target stores to buy a carload of groceries and household supplies, and then drove the entire family to the Rockaway, a coastal area in the borough of Queens hard-hit by the storm. Said Kate,

> First we went to a large donation distribution center, but while we were pulling over, people just started running right up to our car, pleading with us for supplies. So, after that first day, we stocked up again, and we started going to other areas on our own, where we would set up a table and pile it up with supplies, mostly baby clothes and diapers. People just stopped by to pick up what they needed. It was really upsetting to see all the destruction and to realize

how desperate the people there were; it was so close to our home, but it looked so entirely different. The entire area looked impoverished; there was lots of fire damage and water damage. The people we saw looked like they had no homes—and many of them *had* actually lost their homes from the storm's destruction.

Driving the hour or so back and returning from there to our apartment—which was untouched by the storm—was very disconcerting, very upsetting; it was shocking to think how quickly and how totally people's lives had changed so close to where we lived. It drove home to me how devastating the impact of the storm was on the lives of all those people and how much need there was for help. So much of what I feel today about helping other people in even simple ways is a result of what I saw at that time.

COMMUNITY SERVICE

Many schools incorporate volunteerism into the school year through organized community service projects or community service days; they may even make it a requirement to complete a certain number of service hours to graduate. Some schools require that student council representatives and members of honor societies participate in community service. Sometimes students are given an opportunity to select a community service activity from a list, and sometimes an entire class—or even the entire school—might participate in the same activity on the same day. If your school has a requirement to perform a certain number of hours of community service each year or complete a cumulative number by graduation, make sure you know the requirements and develop a plan to fulfill them. When your school offers community service experiences, it is a good way to find out how you feel about volunteering and what types of volunteer experiences there are.

Evan E.'s first experience as a volunteer was in fifth or sixth grade, when his class went to a local elementary school to play with kids with special needs. "It was gratifying," he said, and as his mother pointed out, "Working with young kids eased them into volunteering. It was something familiar to them, and since they did it as a group, it made it easier for them."

As part of the community service program, some schools incorporate classroom time as well, where students discuss and develop projects, and report on them. They may have speakers come in to talk about volunteerism or the organizations with which they are affiliated. Some schools suggest or require that students keep a journal of their experience or write an essay about it. They may have a scheduled debriefing session where students can share their stories and reflections, and discuss concerns. Some students find such writings or reflection meaningful and even use it to develop formal essays for college applications. Other students, however, might find such introspection less helpful or be frustrated to find that classmates might not have taken it as seriously as they did. Sofia had some good insight into her experience with the process of reflection at her school:

> Sometimes, when we had to speak about our experiences during a reflection session, it ended up just being obligatory. I felt that reflection should produce some profound thoughts, but some people just wanted to get it over with. A few times it was a pretty shallow discussion, not really meaningful at all. I thought it would be better if we had someone, maybe an outside speaker, who was committed to service and who knows about service, come up with discussion questions and guide a more worthwhile conversation. It's hard sometimes for people my age to have a deep conversation, but if it was guided, it might be more productive. If someone says something interesting, for example, someone should ask them to fill in more about it, take the discussion further. And I also felt that writing on your own time could be helpful, but sometimes when the reflection session included writing in the classroom, you just want to get it over with.

There are times when community service is *not* a volunteer experience. On some occasions, a judge may sentence a defendant to participate in a certain number of hours of community service instead of (or in addition to) receiving a jail term or fine. The work someone does for required community service may not otherwise differ from that performed by a volunteer.

Whether the initial exposure to volunteerism comes through family engagement or organized community service through school, it often leads to a deeper commitment to helping others. After Sofia had gone for several years to a local soup kitchen to help prepare and serve Thanksgiving dinner, she realized, "I didn't want to forget about these people after Thanksgiving." That led her to write an opinion piece for her school newspaper about "how people just show up for one day and they're all excited about helping society but then end up not continuing." She feels that continued experience as a volunteer develops and nourishes feelings of empathy, and this deepened her commitment to volunteering. She now teaches music to underprivileged kids every Saturday through the music department at her school and also gives a few hours a week at a volunteer-run community bookstore.

SERVICE LEARNING

Some schools incorporate what is called "service learning" into the school year. This is generally a curriculum-based program where students learn by studying a real-life problem in their community and taking action to solve it. Service learning builds understanding of social issues, as well as real-life skills, and involves group planning, discussion, action (service), and reflection.

INTERNATIONAL VOLUNTEERING OR "VOLUNTOURISM"

While it is true that volunteers do not get paid, there are some volunteer opportunities for which *you* have to pay. One of these is what is now labeled "voluntourism," a combination of volunteerism and tourism, where you pay a fee to an organization to travel, usually to a foreign country, to work as a volunteer. Voluntourism trips, often overseas, offer a chance to travel, as well as engage in community service. While there, the agency sponsoring the excursion usually includes visits to tourist sites and offers educational opportunities or the chance to spend time with local residents. It is a combination of service and vacation travel—and usually comes with a significant fee, although sometimes it is possible to receive discounted fares or even grants or scholarships to help fund such a trip. Voluntourism has become a big industry, and some trips are much better organized, supervised, and coordinated than others. Many are sponsored by a school and accompanied or guided by skilled teachers, and include a rigorous educational experience and a meaningful volunteer component. If you are considering such a trip, make sure you research it well and, if possible, speak with people who have taken the trip previously.

Sam was able to experience voluntourism when he paid to go on an organized student travel trip. Although he was able to receive a discount through a family connection, he points out that it was still a struggle for him and his family to be able to afford the international trip. The trip offered an immersive community service and learning experience in a different culture, and most of the students on the trip came from more affluent circumstances than Sam. "I'd had other opportunities to do community service, but this was the first time for many of them to be exposed to doing volunteer work," he said.

> I think a lot of them felt their experience doing this community service in another country was really profound and important, but I think that for me, and for many of the other kids on that trip who were maybe not from such elite backgrounds, the community service we'd done at home, on our own, felt more valuable.

THE INTERSECTION OF VOLUNTEERING
AND CHARITABLE GIVING: THREE SISTERS' STORY

As I wrote about earlier, there is an endless amount of need in the world, and there are endless ways to address it. One of the ways is certainly through charity, defined by Oxford Dictionaries as the "voluntary giving of help, typically in the form of money, to those in need,"[3] whether to an individual or an organization or institution. People give money to help the needy in handouts on the street, collection plates at church, or donation boxes in stores, or by sending checks in the mail or making payments online. These funds help in many ways and, when put to good use, can make an important difference in alleviating suffering.

Volunteering is about giving yourself—your time, your heart, your energy. But many times, volunteering and charitable giving connect. For some volunteers, this is true when they volunteer to collect funds for a cause—you were a volunteer if you ever took a little orange box to "Trick-or-Treat for UNICEF" on Halloween. Almost every weekend, I pass a table set up outside my local supermarket where each week volunteers from different organizations—a high school soccer team, Veterans of Foreign Wars, a church choir, or health-related group—stands behind a jar for coins or a collection box, urging shoppers to contribute.

Similarly, there are collections for *things*: The Lions Club collects used eyeglasses; the local food pantry collects canned goods; the library collects books for their used book sale. These charitable collections serve good purposes, and the volunteers who take the time to organize and staff these collection stations are doing valuable work.

Particularly for young children, learning that collecting money or things to give away to people who need them is a good thing to do and can be a good introduction to volunteering. For one family, that lesson has developed into a family tradition.

Zoe, now fourteen, explained how this tradition began. "It started when I was five years old, and my parents gave me a choice," she said. "I could have a birthday party with presents for myself, or I could collect money for charity instead of getting presents. Every year since then my sisters and I have always been choosing the charities to collect things for instead of getting presents for our birthdays."

Her younger sister, Sophie, now eight, chimed in: "When it was my birthday, I donated socks to the animal welfare league. Animals in shelters are waiting for a home, some are sick, and they don't have homes. The shelter uses the socks to cover bandages or for soft things to comfort them."

Mia, now eleven, told me more.

A teacher at our middle school is also the soccer coach, and he's from Mali. He goes to Mali every year and brings new soccer jerseys to the kids there so they can be ready for soccer. So we collect for soccer jerseys and also collected for shin guards, and he's now turned this into a nonprofit organization to promote soccer in Mali, because he believes being involved in group sports helps the kids there.

Since that first birthday collection the three girls have collected items for a horse rescue organization; dolphin rescue; the local fire department; a homeless shelter; and Paws to Read, a program that brings therapy dogs to the local library for children to read aloud to. Their choices are not arbitrary; the girls carefully select organizations in their areas of interest. For instance, their decision to give to dolphin rescue was made after seeing the movie *Dolphin Tale*. One year, they became interested in helping their local fire department; after calling the department to ask what was most needed, they were told that what the fire station could use was subscriptions to emergency management magazines, because otherwise the firemen would have to pay for those out of their own pockets. In this way, the girls have been able to personalize their charitable intentions in ways that were meaningful to them, as well as the recipients. As Mia explained, "Like when Coach collects soccer things for the kids in Mali; it makes me feel good to think about what we are doing. I really love soccer, and I want those kids to be able to have that experience."

Throughout the years, the girls have also learned more about how to research the organizations in which they are interested, for example, by checking www.CharityNavigator.org, a website that gives information and ratings for various charitable organizations. They write or call the organizations to find out what is most needed and solicit donations for their chosen cause. In this way, they have grown into thoughtful and committed young philanthropists.

Zoe also explained a related concept that has caught the interest and attention of many young people, the kindness project, for which individual kids or entire schools have initiated specific ways to perform acts of kindness. "For my Bat Mitzvah, I chose to do a kindness project," Zoe said.

> I passed out bracelets that said, "Be Kind, and Pass It On," and started a website for it where people could write about what they did to be kind to someone else or about how someone was kind to them. They can go to the web page to write about the kindness that was done. I wanted to try to spread the idea of doing kind things.

The girls went on to tell me how their school is also active in promoting charitable collection activities. In recent years, the school has sponsored a hurricane relief drive, a food drive for a local pantry, and a drive for school supplies. The students at their school, as in many other schools, are also encouraged to collect box tops from breakfast cereal and other packaged goods, which the school can redeem for school supplies.

Service projects in general are very much a part of their local school district, said the girls. In past years, they have participated in a Walk to End Homelessness, a Share the Love Food Drive, and trick or treat at a local senior center. This culture of giving back is important to their community and their entire family, said Zoe. She added, "I like to think about how important it is to help others and about how other people feel. For instance, if you see a homeless person, to think about what it would be like if you were in that situation."

Clearly, the message these sisters have learned throughout the years is an important one every volunteer should recognize; as Sophie said, "When you're doing good, it's not about you—it's about the other person."

VOLUNTEERING AS AN INDIVIDUAL

Sometimes, an opportunity you have to work as a volunteer for one day—whether with your family, school, or community group—will instill in you an interest to do further volunteer work in a similar (or even the same) field or organization. Or you may decide on your own that you would like to volunteer somewhere without having had any previous experience. How should you go about pursuing your interest?

GETTING STARTED AS A VOLUNTEER ON YOUR OWN

Whether tutoring children, mentoring teens, renovating housing, restoring public parks, responding to natural disasters, or caring for aging parents and grandparents, those who serve and volunteer are strengthening our communities for America's future.

—*Bill Clinton, forty-second president of the United States*[4]

If you are going along with your family to volunteer, you've already gotten started. And if you are part of a school community service program or a school club whose members volunteer as a group, you're already on the way. But if you are looking for a way to volunteer on your own, there are a number of things to think about. These things will help determine what kind of a volunteer placement might be best for you.

How Much Time Do You Have to Volunteer?

There are many different kinds of opportunities to volunteer, and one of the things you should consider is how much time you can give to a volunteer program. Some volunteer opportunities are only one-day events, for which you commit to helping for several hours on one day only. Others expect a regular, ongoing time commitment, for instance, two to four hours a week for several months or even a year.

Volunteering for a day is an excellent way to explore an interest, learn about your community, join with friends in a fun activity, or support a cause you believe in without making a long-term commitment. Different types of one-day volunteer opportunities include the following:

- A fundraising event like a 5k charity race, where participants ask friends and family to sponsor their run by pledging to give the organization a certain amount of money to participate in or finish the race. Volunteers are often needed to help runners register, give out water or supplies, and direct runners along the route.

- A holiday party at a nursing home or hospital, or a prom at a school for kids with special needs, where volunteers may be needed to entertain, help serve food, or help with setup or cleanup.

- Helping to serve a holiday meal at a homeless shelter or soup kitchen.

- Participating in a literacy event like "Read for the Record" at a local nursery or elementary school.

- A holiday gift drive, where volunteers may be needed to help wrap or distribute donated gifts.

Ongoing, long-term volunteer opportunities offer a chance to learn about a field or the work an organization does. Ongoing volunteer opportunities might include such things as the following:

- Volunteering in a hospital
- Tutoring children in reading or math
- Teaching in a Sunday school
- Leading weekly bingo games at a local nursing home

Whatever type of volunteer opportunity you choose, you should understand that volunteering is a commitment: The organization will expect you to be there at the time for which you sign up and stay for the entire time you commit to being there. Although a volunteer placement is not a *paying job*, it is a responsibility, and volunteers should expect to treat it that way.

Are You Old Enough to Volunteer?

You also will need to know if there is a minimum age requirement to volunteer. There are certainly opportunities for families to work together, even with young children, and for many kids, that is their first exposure to volunteerism. Some volunteer opportunities are available for young people beginning at age twelve, while others will only take volunteers who are older than fifteen; many medical facilities have even higher age requirements. So, as you are considering where you might like to volunteer, make sure to find out whether you are old enough for the opportunity that interests you.

Do You Prefer to Work Alone Or in a Group?

Think about whether you would like to volunteer as part of an organized group or prefer to work on your own. The advantages to working as part of an organized group are that you automatically have a cohort of volunteers to work with and get to know, and who may even become your friends. Also, when a program is organized specifically for a group of volunteers, oftentimes there are well developed guidelines specifying what you will be doing, possibly a handbook or training manual, and an organizational framework that might include an orientation session, regular supervision, or an adult team-leader.

But there can be a downside to working in a group. Sometimes, when a group of volunteers becomes too friendly, the experience turns out to be more social than meaningful. As Sam, a young volunteer who spent time in several different volunteer placements, put it,

> Being part of a group is something that I do value, but some-times it's easy to find yourself spending time there as a social event, rather than what I feel I'm really there for, which is community service. When I do things individually, I tend to be a lot more focused on what I'm doing, and then I get more out of it.

If you work as an individual, there may be different advantages. You may have more opportunities to work directly with the people you are helping. They may be able to get to know you better as an individual than as a member of a group. And that can turn out to have unexpected rewards, as Jeremy found out when he volunteered to go to a nursing home once a week to lead bingo games. "On the first day I went in, it turned out that they didn't really have a lot of people who wanted to play bingo, and there was only one woman who showed up," he remembered.

> So I asked her if she wanted to play a game, and she ended up teaching me to play Rummikub, which I'd never heard of. I ended up going to visit her every week for a year, and I have memories of getting to know her, and it was a great experience. You could tell that she was lonely and so happy to be with someone. I would keep her company, and I was so happy to just be that special person for her, even if it was only once a week.

Working individually, you may have more opportunity to work with a mentor who gets to know you well. Such a relationship can last well beyond your time volunteering, if you make it a point to keep in touch with your mentor. High school volunteers often turn to people who supervised or mentored them for letters of recommendation for college, jobs, or even graduate school applications. But don't expect (or even ask for) a letter of recommendation unless you were an exemplary volunteer: conscientious, diligent, helpful, careful, and interested in learning.

How Do You Find Volunteer Opportunities?

When your school offers community service opportunities, the teacher, counselor, or librarian who organizes the program may be able to help you focus your interest or direct you to resources you can use to learn about available opportunities. Community organizations may post their needs for volunteers in local venues or their own newsletters. The internet, of course, offers a wealth of information about volunteer opportunities, and often you can inquire about further information or apply online. In the "Selected Resources" section of this book you will find a list of suggestions for ways in which to volunteer, which you can pursue by doing some research on your own.

Do You Want to Explore Your Interests or Something New?

Another important factor in choosing a volunteer placement is whether you want to find an area in which you are already interested or even passionate about, or explore a field you want to learn more about or even try because it is very different from your normal routine. Whether it is working with young children, helping the needy, or working outdoors or with animals; or you feel strongly about the environment, literacy, or helping people with disabilities; or you want to meet and work with people who are different from most people you know, thinking about this can help you search for and choose a volunteer experience.

Can You Create Your Own Volunteer Opportunity?

You may also decide to create your own volunteer opportunity, which has its own rewards. Emily and her sister participated in a local holiday gift drive at a hospital, for which they put together gift bags filled with items requested by underprivileged families. To the girls' surprise, they found that rather than asking for toys or clothing, families listed such basic necessities as toilet paper or gift cards for groceries. After that experience, the sisters decided that, if people asked for these items for the holidays, they must need them throughout the year as well.

Working diligently for nine months on the complicated details of establishing a tax-exempt organization and raising funding to carry out their idea, they created an organization called Project Hearts to Homes, through which they provide laundry baskets to be distributed by hospitals, filled with basic items for low-income new parents of premature babies. "Most of the person I am today," said Emily,

I learned from Project Hearts to Homes. If there's something to do, I assume I'll do it. I learned that I can't do everything on my own, but I can get a team together and mobilize people. Considering that I've been doing this while I'm in high school, my time management skills definitely picked up. And it improved my basic interactions with people: I learned how to get a message across.

Hannah K. was another young person who created her own volunteer opportunity. "I knew I wanted to work with children," she declared,

and there was a boarding school for children with mental health issues around the corner from my house. I scheduled a meeting with the director of volunteers there, and she interviewed me, and she suggested I come whenever I could and hang out with the children. So I came in every Tuesday, and I planned in advance what I wanted to do with them; sometimes we did crafts projects, sometimes I helped them with homework. It was amazing to spend time with these kids, and I loved it when I'd walk in and they'd be calling out "Hey, Hannah, you're here!"

How Much Involvement Should Your Parents Have?

In many ways, since volunteering is practice for a real job, it is a good idea for you to handle as many of the details as possible. That means researching volunteer opportunities, deciding which opportunities you would like to try for, applying for them, and doing the work itself. This is not to say that you should not have guidance or assistance from your parents. Oftentimes they can help you determine what opportunities might work best for you or answer questions that might come up during the application process; however, this is a chance for you to approach a situation on your own and present yourself in a mature way. Many times, people who recruit or supervise young volunteers want to assess the young person's maturity and self-confidence, and having a parent accompany you or participate in the interview process hinders that determination. So, for example, if you need your parent's help to get you to the interview, ask them to wait for you outside, rather than coming in with you. If you need to call or e-mail the organization or director of volunteers, do so yourself, rather than having your parent make the call or send the e-mail. This will help you to gain experience in speaking with an adult whom you don't know on the phone or contacting them via e-mail, and presenting yourself in a purposeful, direct, and appropriate fashion.

THE APPLICATION PROCESS

Once you've found a volunteer position in which you are interested, chances are you will have to apply for it. This may consist of going to the site where you want to volunteer and filling out a paper application, or you may have to fill out an online application. In general, an application may ask for such information as the following:

- Name
- Address
- Phone number (home and/or cell)
- Age
- School
- Year/grade in school
- Why you want to volunteer at that organization

For some volunteer placements, particularly at medical organizations, more information will be required. Many organizations will ask for your social security number. A social security number is a nine-digit identification number given to U.S. citizens, permanent residents, and temporary working residents that is used to keep track of their earnings and the number of years they work, and entitles them to social security benefits based on those figures. Many children born in the United States get social security numbers when they are born, if their parents request them. If you don't have a social security number, now is a good time to apply for one. If you don't already know your social security number by heart, learn it. This is something you will be asked for many times throughout your life; it is an identification number that is *yours alone*, and you should keep it confidential, except when it is required by a trusted organization. You should keep your social security card in a safe place and not carry it with you, which is why it is important to memorize the number so you always have it on hand.

Some organizations will ask about your citizenship status and may require documentation that you are a U.S. citizen, have a "green card" (a permit that allows a foreign national to live and work permanently in the United States), or are a legal citizen of another country. Be prepared by understanding your status; if you are not sure, ask your parent or guardian.

Hospitals and some nursing homes generally require rigorous medical clearance before you can become a volunteer. You may be required to have a medical examination, either by their medical staff or your own doctor; you may have to provide documentation of up-to-date vaccinations or tuberculosis testing, or list any medications you take. You may be required to get a flu vaccination and any other vaccinations you may be missing or are not current on and take a tuberculosis (TB) test. And for some placements you will be required to take a drug test to make sure that you are not using illegal substances.

For most volunteer work, required documentation and clearances must be complete *before* you become a volunteer, so make sure you allow enough time to have everything done before the date you hope to begin your volunteer service.

You may also be asked to provide a school evaluation by a teacher or counselor; if you are a minor (younger than age eighteen), you may be required to provide permission from your parent or guardian to become a volunteer or permission to have medical screening or any emergency medical services necessary. You will probably be asked to provide an emergency contact number, which may be that of a parent, guardian, or another trusted adult.

Some states require *working papers*, proof-of-age certification for minors younger than eighteen years of age. Generally working papers are for paid employment, but some organizations require them even for unpaid volunteer work. They can be obtained through some school guidance offices or city or state labor departments.

Whatever the application process consists of, be sure to review the application carefully before you send it in, making sure you sign it wherever indicated, and include any documentation or additional material that might be requested. Most nonprofit organizations do not have the time or personnel to follow up on incomplete applications. And remember, the application is usually the first impression you will make on the organization: Be sure you put your best face forward.

THE INTERVIEW

Many organizations require a personal interview before you will be accepted as a volunteer. In general, this will be a face-to-face meeting with a supervisor or volunteer director or coordinator. Some organizations may conduct interviews by phone or even video—Skype, Zoom, or FaceTime—but an in-person interview is usually necessary.

Your interview will probably be the most important impression you make on the organization, so it is important that it be a good impression. Once you have scheduled an interview, *make sure you show up on time.* Nothing leaves an unfavorable impression on an employer more than having someone come late for an appointment, so make sure you allow enough time to get there and not feel rushed. You don't want to appear sweaty, flustered, or apologetic.

Dress appropriately. It is always better to be slightly overdressed than run the risk of being too casual or inappropriately dressed. This is an important interview, and you want to give the impression that you are serious about the opportunity and recognize the importance of what you hope to do. Even if you are interviewing for a position for which you will be "dressing down" on a daily basis, for instance, being a counselor at a summer camp or an assistant in a child care center, for which you might wear shorts and a tee shirt to work, dress up a bit for the interview in more business-like clothes, for example, slacks, a skirt, a neat shirt, and unscuffed shoes. It never hurts to dress more formally than the job requires: For young men, a shirt and tie, and even a jacket, are never inappropriate. For young women, tailored slacks or a skirt, with a blouse, jacket, or sweater, are always a good choice.

Always make sure your appearance reflects good hygiene: No matter what your usual style, when you go for an interview, make sure your hair is neat and your breath and body odor are not liable to be offensive. Keep in mind that, for many—particularly older adults—facial piercings, ear bars, and other hardware, as well as excessive tattoos, are still considered unbusinesslike and even inappropriate, so you may want to consider removing or covering up those that might be a little too unusual for an interviewer.

Make sure you know in advance exactly where you are supposed to be for the interview. If you are not sure how to get there, ask. Know in advance how you will travel to the interview: Will you walk? Do you have to be driven there? If so, do you need to make advance arrangements with a parent or friend? Will you need to take public transportation? If you do, make sure you check schedules and routes, and figure out how much time to allow for transportation.

So, you've arrived on time (even a few minutes before the scheduled time), and you are appropriately and nicely dressed. You may have to wait until you are called in, and you may have to fill out application materials if that hasn't been done in advance. If you were told to bring anything (health information, birth certificate, social security number, school records, etc.), be sure to have the right documents with you.

When you meet the person who will interview you stand up; look them in the eye; smile; and give a firm, quick handshake. If you are not used to doing those things, *practice*. Enlist a parent or friend to practice so that you become comfortable looking someone in the eye and shaking their hand. It is an important skill you will need in the future, and this is a good time to develop a good habit. A limp, soft handshake and averted eyes make most people uncomfortable, and that is not the impression you want to make.

What might an interviewer ask? You might be asked to tell a little about yourself, explain why you are interested in becoming a volunteer, and detail any previous experience you may have had as a volunteer or with a similar organization. You may be asked about school, hobbies, and interests. Be prepared to answer these questions. Before you go for your interview, give yourself some time to think about them and be prepared to talk a little bit about them. An interview is a way for someone to get to know you a little in a short period of time. Be honest and forthright; don't exaggerate and don't puff yourself up—be yourself, but be your *best* self.

Address the interviewer respectfully; use their honorific (for instance, Mr., Ms., Dr.), unless they have asked you to call them by their first name.

Although the interviewer will undoubtedly ask you questions, the interview is also a time when you should ask questions, too. You may want to ask about the organization (although it's a good idea to do a little research in advance so you do know about the organization) and what you would be doing as a volunteer. Ask about the expectations the organization has for volunteers. You may ask about whether there is a dress code and if so, what it is.

Understand the requirements; for instance, an organization usually expects a volunteer to be present on a regular schedule. Make sure you know what the schedule is—*and make sure you can commit to that schedule*. Do not say you will be able to maintain that schedule if you know you cannot. If an organization expects a four-month commitment and you know that you've signed up for the basketball team and practice starts in three months on the same day you're expected to volunteer, speak up and tell the interviewer about the conflict. They may be able to make some accommodation, or you may have to come to a decision about which is more important to you—going out for the basketball team or becoming a volunteer for the organization.

When the interview is finished, stand again, shake the interviewer's hand once again, and thank them for taking the time to interview you.

After the interview, write a brief note or e-mail, once again politely thanking the interviewer and expressing your interest in becoming a volunteer. If you have any questions after the interview, this is a good time to ask them as well, and it usually ensures that the interviewer will get back to you.

FOLLOWING UP

You may find, at the end of the interview, that you are told you are accepted as a volunteer. More likely, you will be told that the organization or interviewer will get back to you to let you know. If that is the case and you have not heard from them in a week or two (unless they have told you when to expect to hear from them), you may call or e-mail to inquire as to whether you have been accepted or they might need additional information. One call or e-mail is generally acceptable; multiple, increasingly anxious follow-ups are generally more annoying to an organization than helpful. Use good judgment in deciding how to follow up.

ORIENTATION AND TRAINING

Once you are accepted and ready to start, there will probably be an orientation or training session. Depending on the size and formality of the organization, this may be a large group session with a volunteer manual, handouts, videos, and presentations. For less formal situations, it may take the form of having a supervisor—or even a more experienced volunteer—take you around and show you the ropes. Whichever it is, listen carefully, ask questions, take notes if appropriate, and make sure you know what you are—and are *not*—supposed to do. Many organizations assign experienced volunteers to "mentor" a new volunteer for the first day or first few days; it's a great way to get to know someone who will be working with you. Keep in mind that among the most important things to know are to whom you report and to whom you should go if you have a question.

PART II

EXPECTATIONS AND CHALLENGES

CHAPTER THREE

WHAT MAKES A SUCCESSFUL VOLUNTEER?

America is blessed with millions of individuals of goodwill and good works who play significant roles in making positive change in the lives of others. . . . Many of society's greatest problems can only be solved on a personal level, between those who care and those in need.
—George W. Bush, forty-third president of the United States[1]

WHAT DO SUPERVISORS SAY MAKES A SUCCESSFUL VOLUNTEER?

Many of those who supervise volunteers with whom I spoke indicated that perhaps the most valuable asset in a volunteer is a genuine interest in the cause, the people, and the job they are doing. Other qualities volunteer directors look for include having an open mind and being accepting of people and their diversity. One volunteer coordinator I interviewed told me she urges volunteers to keep their eyes open. Furthermore, what she looks for in a prospective teen volunteer, she told me, is not so much maturity, but a sense of self-reliance, an ability to be somewhat independent, and to be able to problem solve on their own. The most important quality she looks for in a prospective volunteer, she said, is enthusiasm and excitement to be a volunteer.

Marc, who selects and mentors high school volunteers in a hospital, described what he called, the "best kids." He continued, "They're so smart, so aware of everything that's going on. They're motivated, they make contacts in the medical field, and they're so proactive. They really want to get involved and are motivated to find out everything they can from their experience here." Furthermore, he said, "They should have genuine interest in being a volunteer—they shouldn't just be checking off a box on the list of things they should do. When choosing volunteers, I value enthusiasm more than previous hospital experience and try to choose kids who will make the most out of their experience."

The people who supervise teen volunteers have other thoughts on what makes a successful volunteer. One thing most of those I spoke with reiterated is how important it is for a volunteer to be reliable. It is important to understand that even though you are not being paid, being a volunteer can carry just as much responsibility as paid employment. As one coordinator explained,

> We have a limit on how many volunteers can sign up for one shift—our space is small, and if we have too many volunteers, it's too crowded. But our placements are very much in demand. So, if someone signs up for a shift and then doesn't show up, it means that they've taken a slot that another volunteer could have used. It's not fair, and it's discourteous and causes someone else to suffer.

Cheryl, another supervisor, pointed out another particular issue she has with young volunteers: sometimes it seems they forget what they are there to do. Said Cheryl,

> It's important for volunteers to stay engaged with the people they are there to help, to understand that they are not there for themselves. Sometimes I've seen a volunteer get so caught up in an arts and crafts activity that they are not engaged with the client at all and I need to remind them what their goal and purpose is.

Sometimes, particularly as you are getting used to a volunteer placement, you might find that you are uncomfortable in a situation. Being uncomfortable, exploring your feelings about being uncomfortable, and identifying what made you uncomfortable helps you understand and grow, and can make your time as a volunteer a more valuable and successful emotional and educational experience. As one volunteer coordinator suggested to high school students she counsels about volunteering, "Get out of the neighborhood, get out of your comfort zone. Make yourself uncomfortable—and then let's talk about it."

A TIP FROM FELISSA

Felissa, who began volunteering when she was quite young, has this advice for new volunteers: "If you're nervous about going by yourself, go with a friend who'll take it seriously, not just fool around. Keep in mind that people are really glad you're here. It's not something you'll regret, and it will open your eyes and can open so many different doors to so many opportunities."

WHAT DO VOLUNTEERS SAY MAKES A SUCCESSFUL VOLUNTEER?

"Try to have as few expectations as possible. Don't think you're going in to sort of 'save the day,'" advised Hannah A.

> It's not about that. I actually learned more about myself than I did about other people. If you're looking to learn more about yourself, it's a pretty darn good way to do it. Especially for kids and teens, who are very, very programmed to seek success, who expect immediate gratification, volunteering can sometimes be that, if you're lucky, but it's important to learn that, in and of itself, this is what life is like.

"Get moving. If you see something to do, just do it. You'll find it's worth it. If you feel really passionate about something, don't wait: find a way to get involved," said Emily.

Meghan suggested, "Try your best. Remember to follow instructions; if you need help, ask, because when issues come up, it's better to be safe than sorry."

Working in a soup kitchen, Sofia found the following:

> It can be hard to deal with someone who's homeless or someone who may be mentally unstable. You have to have the skills to communicate with them, maybe to get them to calm down or to understand what they want. There isn't necessarily a solution to that, except to try and make them happy if you can, and to try to satisfy what you think their needs are. Don't look down on them, try not to think about how much they need and how much worse off than you they may be in material resources. Just be there with them.

Being open to the potential of being uncomfortable can make a huge difference in the success of a volunteer experience. Isabella, who spent time working as a volunteer in a hospital, says, "Don't be afraid to take that step out of your comfort zone." Generally a shy, reserved person, she says she doesn't like change. It was a big step for her to try working at a hospital, but she found she grew in the sense of not being so afraid to try new things. "I found a sense of independence," she continued. "I found I don't have to rely so much on other people."

"Don't only focus on something you're comfortable with. When you're not comfortable is when you learn the most. Pique your interest. Broaden your focus. Look at a wide array of different opportunities. And try to volunteer with a wide array of different organizations," counseled Cheyenne.

Kristina echoed much of what other volunteers have said. "Keep an open mind," is her first recommendation. "Get out of your comfort zone; volunteer with people you don't usually have an opportunity to interact with or know much about."

"Don't worry about perfection," advised Sofia. "Don't worry about doing everything to your maximum capacity. Mainly, be adaptable to the situation. The important thing is to work with other humans, to learn that it's not just you in the world; know that there are other people with other needs."

"The key to volunteering," said Elizabeth, "is you've got to do something you enjoy."

DEALING WITH PROBLEMS AND CONCERNS

While there is a lot to be said for discomfort as a path to growth and understanding, occasionally you may be confronted with problems that need to be dealt with during your volunteer experience. Part of learning how to be a successful volunteer is learning how to deal with such situations. For example, while you may have been given specific instructions by your supervisor about issues that may arise, not every situation can be anticipated, and you may have to deal with something unexpected. While it is therefore important to keep in mind the information and training you have been given, you may also have to call upon your own good sense, thoughtfulness, and caution to deal appropriately with what you face. It also bears repeating that if there is someone to ask for help or explanation, do so—training volunteers and understanding their predicaments is very much a part of a supervisor's role. But learning how to deal with uncomfortable situations is probably going to be part of your own education as a volunteer. Similarly, being confronted with people who are different from you, whether in financial position or ability, or age, language, or culture, can be fraught with unsettling feelings.

Anna works in the rehabilitation unit of a large metropolitan hospital, where she helps the therapeutic recreation specialists with activities for patients who have suffered spinal cord or traumatic brain injury and have mobility impairments. It can be overwhelming, particularly at first, to see people who have suffered devastating injuries or lost motor function in parts of their body and are learning how to manage in their new situations. It can be an exercise in empathy

Anna volunteered at the rehabilitation unit of a hospital.

and understanding for a young volunteer to find ways to connect on a personal level with people in those circumstances, but it can also foster emotional maturity. In the rehab unit, where many of the patients have limited abilities to speak, Anna had to find ways to communicate and connect with them that she had never anticipated. "You don't know what to expect," Anna pointed out. "But putting a smile on your face is always a good thing. Show respect. Try to be open. It's a good feeling to be able to help them."

WORKING AS A HOSPITAL VOLUNTEER WITH DISABLED PATIENTS: ANNA'S STORY

Anna started her volunteer experience working as a teaching assistant at her after-school Chinese school when she was a freshman in high school. She had graduated from the Chinese school the year before and wanted to give back, so she went to the principal to see what she could do. He suggested she become a teaching assistant for the first through seventh grades. As an assistant, she helped the teachers make copies, teach the youngest kids, and grade papers, and she enjoyed helping the younger kids. Anna worked there for three months but then found that it interfered with tennis and track and had to give it up.

When she was fifteen, her father, who works at a major city hospital, suggested she look for a summer volunteer position there. She researched volunteer opportunities online and got in touch with the volunteer coordinator. Anna completed the extensive application paperwork, which included a school evaluation, medical screening, and getting the required vaccinations. When she received word that her application had been cleared, she went for an interview with the volunteer coordinator and learned she had been accepted into the program and assigned to work with the therapeutic recreation team in the rehabilitation unit.

Anna had to participate in an orientation session, where she learned about how to protect against the spread of infection and introduce herself to patients and make conversation, what she would be expected to do, and what she was not allowed to do. She watched videos about maintaining patient confidentiality and emergency safety precautions, and got to meet the other summer volunteers with whom she would be working. She was introduced to the therapeutic recreation specialist who would be her supervisor and toured the rehabilitation unit, which, in addition to patient rooms, included a physical therapy gym, an occupational therapy gym, and an activity room.

Anna's schedule that summer was to work from 4:00 PM to 6:00 PM three days a week from late June until the second week in August, when she had committed to starting training for the tennis season at school. She had discussed that schedule in her initial interview with the volunteer coordinator to make sure that it would be acceptable.

Anna's job was to assist the therapeutic recreation specialist in preparing and participating in activities that were both recreational and therapeutic. The patients in the rehabilitation unit had suffered traumatic brain injury, spinal cord injury, and strokes; there were also patients who had undergone leg amputations or major orthopedic surgery. What they had in common was that they were receiving intensive physical and occupational therapy to improve their mobility and strength and learn to adjust to assistive devices and techniques they would need to function with newly impaired abilities.

Starting just before July 4, Anna and the other volunteers spent their first day at the hospital preparing and distributing flyers to inform patients of upcoming activities in the therapeutic recreation activities room. They went room to room to invite patients to the activities room, getting an introduction to these severely disabled patients. They saw patients who were paralyzed from the waist down, patients in wheelchairs, patients with missing limbs, and patients who were unable to speak because they were on ventilators after being paralyzed from below the neck. It was an eye-opening and disconcerting experience.

"Going to the first couple of rooms was scary," Anna confesses.

But I was with another volunteer, and that made it a little easier. After the first couple of rooms, we had a really great experience with one guy who was really glad to have us visit, and we got to talking with him and he told us about how he was learning to use a motorized wheelchair, and he was really cheerful. He was young, and he'd had an accident on his motorcycle and broken his back, and he would never be able to walk again, but he had a really positive attitude, and after that, we felt more prepared to visit the other rooms.

We did a lot of activities that summer with the patients. There was a little kitchen at one end of the activities room, and sometimes we would have a cooking class and make things like stuffed peppers or fruit things; some of the patients were able to sit at the table and work with their hands, but others couldn't even move their hands, so we would sit next to them and kind of do it for them or with them. We'd talk cheerfully about what we were doing and just try to keep them engaged in the activity.

Sometimes we would play Wii with them; some of the guys would really get into baseball or golf—Wii was something they could do with very limited hand movement, even from a wheelchair.

One really cool activity was that every Thursday a retired dancer from the Rockettes would come. She would hand out gloves with taps on the palms—because the patients couldn't actually tap dance—and she'd put music on and teach the patients to tap on wooden boards, and they'd put on a show. It was hilarious—everyone would be laughing hard and trying to keep time with the music.

We were never told specifics about how to react to the patients; some of the patients have severely impaired motor function, and some, especially with traumatic brain injury, can have communication difficulties or even behaviors that might be inappropriate but they can't help. And we just tried to be nice, be friendly, to try to communicate as much as we could, just try to connect in a good way with them. Because there were other volunteers my age and we spent the whole summer together, it made for a really comfortable environment, and we really became friends and felt like even on the difficult days, we were all in it together.

I had started to think, even before that summer, that I might want to go into some area of the health field. But working in the hospital that summer was a really great experience, and I am thinking now that I might want to go into nursing or physical therapy. I had a chance to see some really terrific therapists, and what I got to see and hear from them and the patients gave me a sense of what it might mean to do that as a career. So the summer was really, I think, taking a step in the direction I might want to pursue. I'm really glad I had the chance to do it, and I'd say if you're ever given that kind of a chance, take it. You don't know where it will lead.

In almost any circumstance, positivity on the volunteer's part is a useful tool. "Sometimes someone I'm working with might not really want to be there," said Jeremy about his work tutoring elementary school kids in math. "So I have to make that person's experience into a positive one. Sometimes there aren't enough resources to do what I need to do, but I can usually find a way to work around that."

Sometimes a volunteer may find themselves confronted by a situation they don't know how to handle and can't find a supervisor or more experienced volunteer. Jeremy's advice is, "When it's just you and you're in a situation where the supervisor is not with you, you have to just stay calm, do what needs to be done."

Communication is key, many volunteers find. "If there's a problem with something you've been asked to do or you'd rather do something else," said Felissa, "talk to the leader, or the coordinator. They will try to do anything they can to help you; they're there for you to get the most out of your time. Speak up!"

"Some people might hesitate to volunteer," Hannah K. related.

They don't exactly know what it means to volunteer or are afraid of not knowing what they're supposed to do. I think that's what intimidates people the most; they think, "I don't know what to do" or "I don't know how this works or where I'm supposed to go." My advice for that is don't be afraid to reach out to people.

SPECIFIC TIPS FOR BEING A SUCCESSFUL VOLUNTEER

BE ON TIME

It is your responsibility to be present during the time for which you have volunteered. Just because you are not being paid for your time doesn't mean you can come and go as you please. People depend on volunteers—whether it is supervisors who expect the volunteers to show up or the people the volunteers are there to help. If you are unavoidably delayed, try to notify someone at the site, and tell them when you expect to arrive.

KEEP TRACK OF YOUR TIME

There may be a formal way of keeping track of your time, for example, electronic sign-in or a physical log book or sign-in sheet. In some volunteer programs, a supervisor will sign off on the hours served. If there is no formal system for keeping track of time served, keep an accurate account of your hours for yourself. Knowing the total number of hours you served will be useful if you want to request a letter documenting your volunteer service to include in college or job applications, or if you request a letter of recommendation from a supervisor. In addition, there are some scholarship or award programs that recognize and even reward volunteers for the number of hours they serve.

TAKE NOTES

Keep a small notebook and pen in your pocket; jot down information you need to remember, names, things you want to look up, and notes about things you find interesting. Don't depend on taking notes on your cell phone—cell phone use is prohibited at some volunteer sites, and you may be asked not to use your cellphone while on duty. Taking notes is both a good way to learn and a resource should you want to write about your experience as a volunteer for a college essay or reflection piece for school.

ASK QUESTIONS

Since one of the goals (one hopes) of being a volunteer is to learn, the best way to do that is to ask questions. Asking questions will help you learn more about the organization for which you are working, the people the organization serves, the neighborhood, and the political or social environment. Learning as much as you can while engaged in a volunteer experience can be the ticket to focusing in on an interest or career direction.

It is also important to ask questions to ensure that you know what you should and should not be doing. Particularly in the beginning, you will probably need to ask a lot of questions to make sure you are doing the right thing. People expect that volunteers will have questions, and most supervisors are eager to answer and educate volunteers. Equally important, they want to make sure volunteers know exactly what they should be doing and become comfortable doing it.

BE OPEN TO AND INTERESTED IN THE PEOPLE AROUND YOU

One of the greatest benefits of being a volunteer is the opportunity to spend time with and learn from people outside your usual circle. Be open to that experience; listen to people—it's more important to hear from them than to talk about yourself.

BE WILLING

Being a volunteer means you are willing to help—so be willing to help in any way you can and let people know you are. Being alert, looking interested, offering to help are ways you can convey that you want to be useful. Being a willing and engaged volunteer will make people notice and remember you in a positive fashion, and that can pay off in not only making your own experience more meaningful, but also receiving more meaningful and complimentary service letters or letters of recommendation.

CHAPTER FOUR

WHAT YOU LEARN
AS A VOLUNTEER

Through the dedicated efforts of America's volunteers,
we are building a culture of service, responsibility,
and compassion, particularly among our young people.
—George W. Bush, forty-third president of the United States[1]

Self-confidence. Leadership. Time management. Communication skills. Problem-solving. Self-awareness. Compassion. Empathy. These are some of the valuable skills you can gain as a volunteer; however, there are other, more subtle but no less important things volunteers may learn as well. For some young volunteers, it is the recognition of the comforts of your own life or of the fact that your struggles are relatively insignificant compared to those of some people. This provides important lessons because doing volunteer work often brings you into contact with people whose lives are very different from your own.

Hannah A. first volunteered as a young teen, working at a day care center in a shelter for young mothers and their kids. "I think that at that time in anyone's life, especially if you're privileged enough to be thinking these things, you're wondering, who am I? What am I doing here?" she said.

> Typical teenage kind of stuff. And I think it's helpful, or at least I found it was helpful, to be given a window into a world that was so vastly different than mine; it was an extraordinary opportunity.

I learned more about myself than I did about other people. And I learned that if you're looking to learn about yourself, it's a pretty darn good way to do it. And I think the most important thing I learned is that if you go in feeling that you're going in to save people, that's just not going to happen. You have to know that you're going there to be their friend, not their savior, to be there *with* them, as opposed to being there *for* them. And that takes the pressure off, in a good way.

Hannah continued,

Sometimes it's the little things that are so good. I worked for a long time with a middle schooler who just didn't seem to connect with me. But one day, when I came in, he gave me a Hershey's Kiss, and that was amazing, it felt like a breakthrough. Especially for kids, teens, and young adults, who are very, very programmed to seek success in their grades, in all their activities, they are looking for instant gratification. Volunteering can be that, sometimes, if you're lucky, but I think it's important to learn that, in and of itself, this is what life is like.

Being able to interact with people whose circumstances are less fortunate than your own can be an extraordinary way to rethink your own situation and gain a new perspective. "Many of the people that I interacted with at the hospital were old," Afsana remembered.

And they appreciated my company, and I appreciated their trust. Being the oldest and coming from a very low-income family, a lot of times I would think that my life was the only misfortune, but I was wrong. My problems were minuscule compared to what many people I saw went through, and I learned to appreciate my life the way that it is. Every day I would go home inspired or sad but always adding something to my philosophy about life.

Seeing the world and the people in it from a different perspective can be an invaluable opportunity for a young volunteer. One high school student, who was able to travel abroad with a school volunteer program, wrote, "Having the chance to go to Haiti with a group to volunteer was a window into a whole new world. It gave me a lot of perspective. I feel like my classmates and I have grown up in a bubble of opportunities, and this trip allowed us to understand about those not as fortunate."

Anna, who volunteers in a hospital rehabilitation unit for patients with spinal cord injuries and traumatic brain injuries, many of whom will never regain the ability to walk, talk, or even breathe independently, succinctly summed up her takeaway: "I learned to be grateful for my health and to be thankful for my life."

Sometimes volunteering can help you focus on career goals. Since she was in sixth grade, Meghan has wanted to be a psychologist. That year, she had a teacher who talked about psychology, and that peaked Meghan's interest. Since she's been volunteering with a therapeutic horseback riding program, where she helps children with disabilities learn to ride horses, which helps them improve their balance, confidence, and motor coordination, Meghan realized how much she enjoys working and talking with children. This has reinforced her goal of studying psychology; as she says, "That's the fuel I want to go for!"

In addition to helping her choose a direction for her future, Meghan also found that volunteering helped her with time management; she used to find herself overwhelmed by how to balance her schoolwork and after-school activities as a Girl Scout, student, and volunteer. But she's learned to keep a structured calendar and check it regularly, and now she plans the days when she can volunteer based on how her calendar shapes up.

And, Meghan said, volunteering can be therapeutic in its own way. When she's stressed about school or her busy weekends, her work with children and horses takes her mind off school or the pressures of her busy days and helps her forget her stress.

"I worked in a hospital, feeding patients, talking with patients, helping them," Bella related.

It was intense, because you're dealing with someone's life, and it was overwhelming and freaked me out at first. But once you're in the moment, when I got more used to it, I got more comfortable with it. It may not be for everybody, but overall it was very fulfilling; there was sometimes instant gratification. You do something, people are grateful, even if it's just bringing them water. I'd had other volunteer opportunities, doing meal preparation for God's Love We Deliver, but it didn't have the same impact for me, because there was no direct contact with the people we served. And working in the hospital definitely pushed me further toward nursing; I was able to talk to the nurses, and I learned I definitely do want to work in a hospital.

MIDORI'S STORY: TAKING A CHANCE

One thing volunteers often learn is that they learn as much about themselves as they do about others. Midori is a sophomore who volunteers with a therapeutic horseback riding program. She heard about this volunteer placement from her freshman teacher, who e-mailed students information about different volunteer opportunities. Midori had never been near a horse, let alone on one, but this placement was the one closest to her home, so she applied and was accepted. In the beginning, she said, she was anxious about being near the animals and the young riders' safety. "But I came every Sunday, and little by little, I began to be more comfortable," she revealed. "Each day I learned more and more, and that helped. And I always felt I could go to the instructor or an experienced volunteer, that if I really wanted to know something, I could go to them."

"And I learned that everybody is different, including the horses; everyone has different personalities and moods—and the kids do, too." Midori continued. "The kids who ride in the program have all sorts of physical disabilities, and they go through a lot, day to day, but they come here and there are people who care about them and help them learn new things."

Midori also found that volunteering helped relieve the stress of a difficult academic year. "I took five Regents exams this year, and it was tough," she admitted.

> But interacting with the kids, leading the horses, you focus so much on the horse and the kid riding that you can't focus on how hard the week was and how you went through a lot. So I would say to kids thinking about volunteering, take a risk! If you're not sure about volunteering someplace, make an effort to find out about it; even go there to see. Learning new things keeps you active in life; you won't be doing the same thing every day. So take a chance—because if not, you might feel someday, "I should have done that when I had the chance."

Sam did a stint as a volunteer in New Orleans after Hurricane Katrina, where he helped paint houses for people whose homes were devastated by the floods. At first he found it a little scary and uncomfortable to walk up to strangers' homes and find out what they needed him to do. But as the week went on, he grew more comfortable with it. "I got the absolutely rewarding sense that they were just so happy with what we did; it made me feel happy, and that was the best part of the experience," he declared. "At the end of the day, it's a rewarding feeling knowing that I'm helping people, and that feels good, because I'm not doing it for the money."

"One thing I'm always questioning is, how meaningful is what I'm doing?" Sam continued. "Am I putting my whole heart into it? I want to make sure that the job I'm doing is one I'm doing meaningfully, that I am putting my whole heart into it. So I say, don't try to get anything out of it other than a rewarding sense of knowing that you're doing it with your whole heart."

Being able to give back to something that helped you along the way is also a powerful takeaway from a volunteering experience. Azeem, now a senior, said,

As a high school student, I went back and volunteered at my elementary school, helping teachers grade papers, playing with the pre-K and kindergarten kids, and just helping the school with whatever work they assigned me to. And I realized that I was helping the school with something they may have been unable to do. I was happy to be giving back to the school that helped shape me into the person I am today. It made me realize that volunteer work is not a chore or an assignment; it was an activity I wanted to do. The vice principal made it clear he was very pleased with my work and kept thanking me; it made me feel satisfied and grateful that I was able to do it.

Anna, who volunteered in a hospital, had this suggestion for young people considering volunteering: "You won't know what to expect; just show respect, have a positive outlook—and a smile on your face is always a good thing." "Furthermore," she said, "being in an environment like that, having the chance to work in a hospital was amazing; if you get a chance like that, always take it in—you never know what the next opportunity like that will be."

Another student offered the following reflection on the effect volunteering can have: "It changes people when they do something that's not just for themselves."

Bella had this to say, based on her experience: "Everyone loves volunteers. There are no negatives. You won't lose from volunteering."

And Sam had a perceptive thought about the process of becoming a volunteer, which organizations and agencies that use volunteers should definitely keep in mind when trying to recruit new people: "When you don't have an easy way to volunteer, it's just too easy *not* to volunteer."

Evan, who spent a week as a volunteer in Costa Rica, where he worked with orphans and senior citizens, said he felt "not so much smarter, but like I had a more diverse mind." He added,

I felt more of a global citizen. And it hit home for me when I got back to school, and kids were asking each other, "So what did you do on vacation?" And they were saying, like, "Oh, I was in

Aruba" or "I was sitting on a beach." And then they asked me, and I felt proud to be able to say, "I was in Costa Rica, I was helping people." And that made a difference for me.

For Sofia, "practicing empathy" is a big part of volunteering, as is, she said, "Having compassionate consideration of the situations of others. When we tend to feel sorry for someone, it's taking a judgmental position. But empathy puts you on a level playing field, where you can try to make a real connection with someone, in that moment."

"I would tell someone who is looking to volunteer or who wants to learn more about volunteering that you have to go in there with a positive attitude," said Jeremy.

You're there to be a bright spot in someone's life. You're helping someone out, so you want to be positive. You want to make sure that, if you're working one-on-one, you're not being too pushy. You're giving them the help they need but without being overbearing. Be as helpful as you can be, like if you're working with a group putting together care packages for people, try to be the one who takes action, who says, "I'll get this supply, or I'll cut here," or whatever needs to be done. I guess positivity is the number-one thing.

"From volunteering, I definitely feel that I have become a more helpful person," Jeremy continued. "I want to carry that into my everyday life. I think I've become a more positive person, and also maybe it's made me a little bit more vocal, a little bit more of a leader, and better at communication."

Having a good supervisor can be important. "It helps when the leader is supportive, active in educating the volunteers," said Elizabeth. "When the place where you're working has a good support system for the volunteers, it can make all the difference. Putting yourself in a place with a good support system, you can learn how to deal with situations a little better."

Elizabeth volunteered as a teaching assistant at a school for children on the autism spectrum. Even though she has a brother with autism, she stated,

Evan was an international volunteer in Costa Rica, where he called out
Bingo numbers in Spanish and played with orphans.

There is such a difference among those on the spectrum; I saw all sorts of things I'd never seen before. One of the kids had a feeding tube because they couldn't eat by mouth—my brother would eat all the time if he could. One of the kids was extremely violent; one wouldn't take a nap. I thought I knew what to do because of my personal experience, but these kids were completely unlike my brother. But the teachers I was working with knew what to do, knew how to react, and walked me through it. That was extremely helpful.

ELIZABETH'S REFLECTIONS ON HER GROWTH AS A VOLUNTEER

Elizabeth's experience as a volunteer was, in many ways, emblematic of that of many young volunteers. "Volunteering was always something in the curriculum and in my family," she said. Her school incorporated community service activities into even the youngest grades, and Elizabeth often joined her family in preparing and serving meals at a local food pantry. When she got to high school, Elizabeth chose to spend one summer working four days a week as a volunteer teaching assistant at a school for children on the autism spectrum. She commented,

> My brother is on the autism spectrum, and I felt it was something I knew about and had experience with. When I started there as a volunteer, I was somewhat restricted in what I could do because there was always a teacher and other teaching assistants to do most of the work. But they provided a support system for me, which is integral, because the adjustment to working with a very disabled population can be hard—almost impossible—to do, unless there's a mentor who can help explain things and make sure you know what to do. I thought I knew a lot about kids on the spectrum, but these kids were so different from what I knew. There was a lot that was intimidating to me

at first—behaviors and physical things that I hadn't seen before and wasn't sure how to handle. I learned a lot from the teachers and teaching assistants, and I realized, after being there for a while, that there was a lot more that I could handle and really help with than I'd expected.

That experience also colored Elizabeth's future choices in volunteerism. She stated,

I realized that working in a school like that, it's very different from when you work in a food bank or a shelter kitchen. When you volunteer in a soup kitchen, for example, you are giving out meals to many people, and you see the people there for maybe an hour or two, but then they walk away and you don't have a chance to develop relationships the way you do working regularly in a classroom. And I realized I liked that feeling, that I was really getting to know somebody as an individual. I know a lot of people volunteer to serve meals at a soup kitchen, or help clean a church, but I found what I really do best, and what's most important to me, is to work one-on-one with someone.

After high school, Elizabeth continued to find volunteer opportunities that were important to her. During college, she found a volunteer position working with Autism Speaks, a major national nonprofit dedicated to autism awareness and advocacy, where she helped connect families with appropriate resources. "I had a wonderful supervisor there, someone who was really supportive in educating volunteers, and that was a terrific experience; she really taught me a lot," she remembered.

Reflecting on her school days as a volunteer, Elizabeth had another valuable observation to make about how important awareness and education is in terms of opening your eyes to the needs of the community. She explained that when she was in high school, she'd seen the movie *Same Kind of Different as Me*, about the interactions between a middle-class family and a homeless man, and it made a big impression on her. Not long thereafter, her high school hosted a panel discussion with some homeless and formerly homeless people, who talked about their experiences with homelessness. She said it was powerful and brought the issues of homelessness much more to light for her and her classmates. "Learning in depth about an issue and actually meeting and talking to people who experience it is a tremendous opportunity, and gives you insight into things you might do to help alleviate suffering and really help people," she stated. "I think every volunteer opportunity should help open your eyes like that."

Gabriel supervises volunteers for a program that produces in-house television shows for pediatric patients at a major city hospital. He works with five high school students who work on weekends, putting together three live television shows a day. Volunteers in his program create new programming, update programming, and produce and host interactive shows in which patients can participate from their beds. Since the volunteers work in a professionally equipped television studio, they have the opportunity to learn to use sophisticated technology and equipment. For students who are interested in pursuing careers in communications or broadcasting, this is a huge advantage; they are steps ahead of most beginning college students.

Sometimes student volunteers gain experience facing emotionally or psychologically stressful situations. In Gabriel's work with high school volunteers in the hospital setting, he is careful to prepare the volunteers for what they might face. Because they will be interacting with very sick children, many who are bedridden with an intimidating array of tubes and other medical equipment, he also teaches the volunteers the procedural protocols, privacy and confidentiality rules, and safety requirements they must know. He explains to volunteers how dire the medical situations they may be faced with are and how to respond in an emergency. He makes sure they understand that while it can be a daunting and emotionally stressful environment, they should be mindful that they are there to help, provide relief, and bring a smile to someone's face. He encourages volunteers to recognize the positive difference they are making, providing smiles and a distraction to sick children and their families.

And Gabriel encourages the volunteers to discuss how they feel about difficult situations they may have faced in their work. Being able to talk about their feelings and process their experiences makes them better able to handle them, learn from them, and be prepared for the next time they are confronted with something similar.

Based on her experience working with disabled young riders, Cheyenne found herself mentally rejecting stereotypes she'd had. She grew to understand how much more there was to learn about understanding people. She needed to become more knowledgeable, intuitive, and compassionate—and she was learning this because of her work with not only children, but also animals. She began to understand the multifaceted ways we can communicate and show feelings without words or conventional methods. From the young riders, she learned how they communicated with eye movements and facial gestures when they couldn't communicate with words. She began to recognize how body language could convey nervousness or confidence. She learned how to recognize the body language of the horses as well and when to anticipate based on their movements whether they might become agitated, which allowed her to keep a serene environment so neither rider nor horse would get agitated.

She also learned the importance of teamwork. In one instance when she was leading a horse being ridden by a little girl with cerebral palsy, the rider became frightened and started to make bouncing movements, which began to upset the horse. Cheyenne knew she couldn't let go of the horse to help the child and realized she needed quick and effective teamwork to keep the situation safe. But the volunteers she was working with that day were new and didn't have enough experience to know what to do. Thinking quickly and communicating calmly with the volunteers to instruct them what to do, Cheyenne was able to ensure the safety of the rider.

Felissa has spent years as a volunteer with Gliding Stars, a program that teaches children with motor disabilities how to ice skate. "I learned a lot about how different people react to changes and how to adapt to things," said Felissa.

> When the coordinator of our program left and a new coordinator came in and changed basically everything, some of the parents of the kids in the program didn't like it and pulled their kids out, and it was kind of a crisis. I learned a lot from watching how the coordinator dealt with it, how she dealt with the parents. She helped me understand that even if kids left, the program would still continue and I shouldn't let it get me down.

Felissa also felt she learned a lot of different ways to talk and interact with different kinds of people. "I feel that now I won't be discouraged from talking to someone if they're different from other people I usually interact with," she acknowledged. "My volunteering expanded my horizons and allowed me to meet and talk to lots of people, and I know I now have more skills in communicating."

GROWING INTO A BIGGER
VOLUNTEER ROLE: FELISSA'S STORY

As so many volunteers do, Felissa, now a seventeen-year-old junior in high school, developed her interest in volunteering through her local house of worship. As a youngster, she attended her congregation's Sunday school. When students complete the fifth grade, they attend Saturday Shabbat (Sabbath) school. While Felissa was attending Shabbat school, she decided she wanted to help out with the Sunday school as well and volunteered to help with the pre-K program there.

"I've always felt I've wanted to help people," Felissa recalled, "even when I was very little."

During her middle school years, Felissa participated in volunteer activities at Second Harvest and the Ronald McDonald House with her mother and sisters. She also helped raise money for several causes through her school.

An avid ice-skater since fifth grade, when Felissa was in junior high school a friend told her about a program in which he participated called Gliding Stars, which has many chapters nationwide and teaches children with physical disabilities how to ice skate using special assistive devices. Each season culminates with the youngsters putting on an annual ice show, with an audience of family and friends to cheer them on.

Felissa started as a general volunteer, joining in the middle of the season. She was paired up with a "Star," one of the disabled students, and skated with them every week, teaching new skills as the youngster developed confidence and ability. "Some of the kids who come don't have any confidence," Felissa recounted. "But Gliding Stars has a motto, 'I can do this, I can skate,' and it's amazing to see how these kids end up with enormous grins on their face as they realize what they can do."

"Kids who are different," Felissa went on, "are constantly told they can't do this, they can't do that; but I've seen kids actually learn to walk and gain confidence and social skills through Gliding Stars."

Since beginning with the program, Felissa has continued for the past six or seven years. Some years she was paired with one person for the entire season, and she loved being able to really get to know each youngster and watch their progress.

As a constant, committed, and engaged volunteer, the program's leadership grew to depend more and more on Felissa, and invited her to participate with board leadership in regular meetings, helping plan programs and training sessions, and discussing the business complexities of running such an organization.

In her years as a volunteer with Gliding Stars, Felissa said she has learned a lot—about organizations, people, and herself. She has seen the program develop and grow, and experienced the changes such growth brings, including changes in leadership, differences of opinion on what directions that growth should take, and how such changes affect the people involved. As the group has grown Felissa has been able to watch—and take an active role—as the program brought in new leadership; became much more structured, with better defined roles and expectations for teachers and coordinators; and developed a better curriculum. She attends board meetings throughout the year and is invited to share her ideas, as well as participate in making decisions about themes, music, and choreography for the annual ice show.

"Overall, it's been a really great experience," Felissa commented.

Teens don't often have the experience of being in business meetings. I feel that my ideas are heard, valued, allowed, and not ignored; I haven't had that experience in other settings, and it's a great feeling. And sometimes I see things differently from the adults—sometimes I even stir up a little fun, a little trouble.

And I've learned a lot about how different people react to changes. Recently, the program hired a new coordinator, someone who basically changed everything—the classes, the way things were done. Some of the parents didn't like it and even threatened to pull their kids out of the program. But I watched how the coordinator handled the parents, explained why the changes were being made, and worked to smooth things over. And I really learned a lot from watching her; it wasn't an easy position for her to be in, but she worked things out. And I think watching that whole thing, learning from how she handled it, will help me deal with situations in the future.

Over the years working with Gliding Stars, I've learned a lot about how to talk to and interact with so many different kinds of people—different from the type of kids at my school. In some ways, people are afraid of trying to communicate with someone who is different. As a teen, I've had so much more experience talking with kids who have different abilities and difficulties communicating, and I've been able to develop skills in how to communicate with them and I know that I won't be discouraged from trying to talk with people who are different in the future. Working with Gliding Stars has definitely helped me expand my horizons and I know will help me in the future, especially because it's made me realize that I want to find a career doing something that will be helpful to other people. I'm thinking about studying special education or even deaf communication. I've been learning American Sign Language (ASL), because when I was in middle school, there was a girl in an afterschool program there who was deaf. Some of the kids made fun of her or just ignored her. I felt like I wanted to be friends with everyone, and I wanted to be able to communicate with her. Someone loaned me a book on sign language, and I learned a few baby signs. In high school, they offered ASL for sophomores, and I took it and really liked it. So, even though that wasn't technically through my volunteer experience, I realize that it all comes from my knowing that I want to help people.

Expanding your horizons is an excellent reason to volunteer, but oftentimes it entails being confronted by circumstances very different than those with which you are familiar. Evan E. found that to be the case when he helped out at a soup kitchen. "Some of the people there are really rough and tough people, and the kids tried to be kind, but sometimes the people they served talked roughly," he described. "It was pretty startling to some of the kids, and they were actually a little scared. But there were also people there who were kind and appreciative. I think the biggest thing that sunk in for us was actually interacting with a lot of people who were not as fortunate as us."

Evan did find, however, that there were some things about the experience that were less appealing than others. When he worked packing foods at a homeless shelter, by the end of his shift his hands smelled pretty bad, and he recalled, "The room smelled like garbage; it was kind

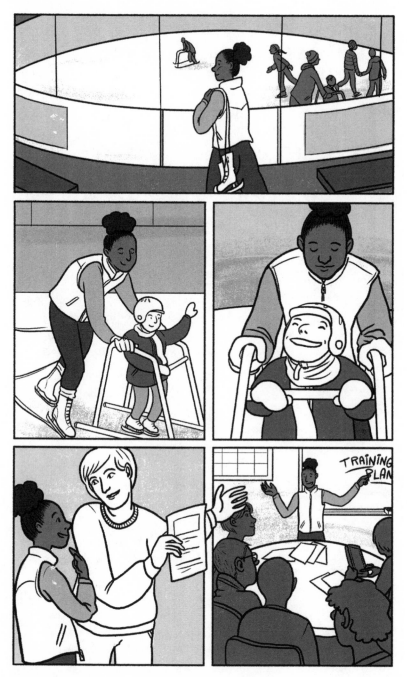

Felissa started as a volunteer with the Gliding Stars ice skating program and was later asked to join the board.

of gross. But the other thing I learned," he continued, "is that it's so easy to help. Any time you give is time well spent; whether it's ten minutes or one or two hours, it gives you a great feeling, and you know you're doing someone good."

"I felt proud to have been given this much responsibility and respect," said one former volunteer. "The staff treated me as a grown-up, and it made me feel more mature. Working in that environment also taught me how to be more emotionally strong and helped me develop a stronger work ethic. I feel that it helped me progress as an individual."

Winnie echoed that feeling: "I was slowly given more and more tasks, and it was a good feeling because I felt like I was being trusted with a bigger responsibility. . . . I felt like I was part of the team."

Young people who volunteer can also learn valuable social skills that they can use and expand on throughout life. It is often a young person's first opportunity to interact with adults on their own—without the structure or comfort of school or family. Learning social cues from the adults they work with can be an informal and often stress-free introduction to a more adult world.

Networking—making connections through social interactions—is another invaluable skill teens can learn from their volunteering experience. The ability to get to know someone and reach out and connect with them based on a common interest, whether it be to get help securing a job or a recommendation for college, internship, or scholarship applications, is a useful skill to have throughout life, and being able to meet and connect with people as a volunteer can yield significant benefits.

Howard, another former volunteer, found that his volunteer experience changed the way he thought about his future. "My dad always urged me to pursue a profession in the field of medicine," he revealed.

I told him that I didn't want to become a doctor; however, this experience as a volunteer has changed the way that I look at hospital work. It's not all blood, death, and despair at every turn in the hospital. There have been spectacular moments when I have seen patients truly gratified by a nurse's work, and this just changed my thought process completely.

On occasion, a volunteer might have the chance to be part of something beyond their typical expectation or duties. Stephen worked as a volunteer in a hospital unit while in high school. "When a doctor saw the curiosity I had for his work, he pulled me into the patient's room and taught me some basic procedures," he said. That is an unusual opportunity and meant a lot to Stephen, who now hopes to become a doctor one day.

Many volunteers find that working with staff can be a tremendous learning opportunity, as well as an unexpected joy. As Julia reported on her experience working in a hospital,

> The staff could not have been more welcoming—within a few weeks, everyone knew my name, and I had daily conversations with all of the nurses, which often ended in laughter. One of the residents even took an interest in me and let me shadow him for an afternoon. Not only did I get to watch him, but he even talked me through everything he was doing. If I had to pick the best day of the whole summer, that might have been my favorite day.

What volunteers learn is not always what they expect they'll learn. "When I first went to work at the hospital, I mainly just refilled the glove dispensers and filled water pitchers," said Rezwan.

> I felt a little bit awkward trying to talk to patients at first because I didn't think they would want to talk to some random seventeen-year-old volunteer, but to my surprise, a lot of them did. I especially remember one patient in her mid-twenties who I talked with for over an hour, and she even attempted to teach me how to knit. I came to find that a lot of the patients really were brilliant people, and I'm sure I got way more out of the conversations than they did. One patient, for instance, taught me more about the Vietnam War than I ever could have learned in school. His stories were so vivid, and it was clearly so important to him to be able to tell them. I don't think I'll ever forget what he told me.

When a volunteer gets caught up in an unexpected circumstance and is able to pitch in and make a positive difference, it means a lot to everyone involved. Jonathan, another hospital volunteer, recounted an extraordinary experience from one evening:

> I'll never forget one night when, right as I was about to finish my shift, a flood of patients poured into the unit. The other volunteer was unable to come in that day because he had a concert, but my friend, another volunteer working in a different unit, had just finished her shift, so she rushed over to our floor to help out. For the next two hours, we scrambled around the unit helping the unit clerk, the nurses, the aides, and the patients in whatever way we could. The unit clerk was the one being hit the hardest by the amount of work, but he kept his cool and got through it all. By the end of our extended shift, we had registered eleven patients and discharged eight. It was a crazy and exhausting night, but from then on, everyone on the floor, the unit clerk especially, never let us forget how thankful they were that we were there that night, and it gave me a real insight to how hectic hospital life can really get.

Volunteers are sometimes able to put to use skills they could never imagine they'll be using. "One thing that was really memorable," said Belinda, "was when I got to practice my Spanish with a patient, who even asked me if I was Mexican! It was surprising and in a sense flattering, but I just loved knowing that my language skills helped make somebody feel more comfortable."

And, as Jeremy reported, you don't always know what you'll end up learning. "I was apologizing to this patient because I wasn't able to help her with something. She said that it's not always the grand gestures that make the most difference, sometimes it's something like learning about a procedure so you can relay it to the patient in a comforting way," he related. "Or, she said, sometimes it's just sitting there with someone watching the *Ellen DeGeneres Show* for a half-hour that makes the most difference."

CHAPTER FIVE

VOLUNTEER CHALLENGES

*America's story has been marked by the service of volunteers. Generations
of selfless individuals from all walks of life have served each other and our
nation, each person dedicated to making tomorrow better than today.
They exemplify the quintessential American idea that we can change
things, make things better, and solve problems when we work together.*
—Barack Obama, forty-fourth president of the United States[1]

While being a volunteer should be meaningful to both the volunteer and the people they serve, there is every reason to expect that it can also be a personally gratifying experience, as well as an enjoyable one; however, there are also often challenges to being a volunteer. It is valuable to recognize this before you become a volunteer and consider how they may impact your experience.

VOLUNTEERS WITH SPECIAL NEEDS

Young people with special needs can also benefit from volunteering. Jennifer, who teaches students on the autism spectrum and with other developmental disabilities, has found that in her experience, while some of her students may not be able to understand the concept of volunteering, "There are skills they are good at and skills they can learn." "Volunteering can teach useful life skills," she said, "and even students who are not able to grasp larger concepts can learn that when they have done a nice thing for someone else, they should feel proud."

Teachers are often those who know what opportunities might be the best for their students. Being able to connect a student's interest with a volunteer opportunity can often spark empathy, understanding, and an active desire to help, even in young people who might not have the same skills and abilities as others.

For instance, teachers who work with young people on the autism spectrum often find that their students have strong affinities for animals. One teacher with whom I spoke explained how several of her students became excited about the chance to do volunteer work for a local cat shelter. Some worked to help socialize abandoned kittens by handling them gently and playing with them. Other students, less eager to deal directly with the animals, helped create a brochure publicizing the benefits of animal adoption.

At an after-school program for other teens on the autism spectrum, the participants worked together to help raise donations for a homeless shelter, as well as an animal shelter. For many such students, these programs offer an important opportunity for "service learning," the chance to develop and improve such practical skills as writing, design, and budgeting, as well as successful teamwork.

At GallopNYC, a therapeutic horseback riding program in New York City, young people with differing abilities are among the many teens and adults who serve as volunteers. Those who are physically able can train as "sidewalkers," walking alongside disabled young riders and helping keep them steady and safe while on horseback, and also helping with horse care and barn chores. Some young volunteers with cerebral palsy, who do not have the mobility or stamina to keep up with the horses, can help with feeding the animals; even those in wheelchairs can load buckets in their laps and are pushed down the barn aisle to distribute feed. Others help with checking in and scheduling, keeping track of students when they arrive and are scheduled to ride, and distributing and fitting helmets on young riders.

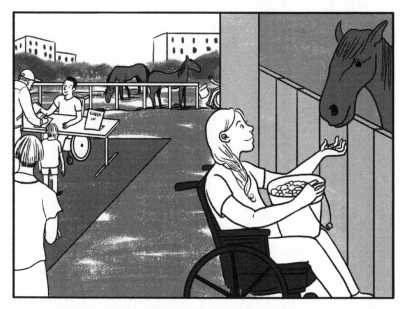

At GallopNYC, young people with differing abilities are among the many teens and adults who serve as volunteers.

Debbie, the mother of a young man on the autism spectrum, told me about her son's experience. As a high school student, he was extremely shy and had social issues that made his high school experience difficult. It was particularly hard for him to go into new situations. He was, however, a talented ice hockey goalie and encouraged to volunteer with a program that teaches disabled children who use all sorts of assistive devices to learn how to ice skate. He was assigned to work with a young boy who was also on the autism spectrum. From the beginning, his supervisor was impressed with his diligence, reporting to Debbie that he worked so hard, he wouldn't even take a break. (But, as her son told Debbie, "I was so afraid to talk to anyone that I just kept working!") But as he began to work regularly with the boy during a period of months, his own confidence grew, and he became more able to navigate social interactions like speaking with the boy's parents and helping the other volunteers.

Debbie had some words of wisdom for supervisors who work with young volunteers with special needs:

> A child with special needs doesn't want to feel like he has special needs. To be invited in, asked to help, to have someone reach out saying, "Can you help us with . . ." goes a long way. It would also be good to follow up with them after they finish their stint as a volunteer, keep them on a list of volunteers, ask them to come back sometime; it will go a long way to making them feel needed and worthwhile.

Debbie also went on to point out, "It's hard to get a first job, and volunteering is a great way toward getting one. My son is now in college and starting to get paying jobs. For him, volunteering was a stepping stone, a way to build his confidence."

Like any volunteers, young people with special needs must be able to demonstrate that they can listen, follow instructions, and be willing to help. They should understand what is expected of them and what they themselves should expect. And like any young volunteers, the benefits for them include the chance to develop teamwork skills, responsibility, and confidence in their own abilities. Particularly for young volunteers who are confined to wheelchairs or have physical impairments that impede their abilities, the opportunity to help others when they themselves are so often the recipients of help from others can be a huge confidence booster. As one supervisor who incorporates volunteers with special needs into a larger volunteer corps pointed out, "Inclusion is good for everyone. Everyone benefits from learning to be respectful of others."

HANDLING PROBLEMS AND CONCERNS

Part of learning how to be a successful volunteer is learning how to deal with difficult situations. For example, while you may have been given specific instructions by your supervisor about issues that may arise, not every situation can be anticipated, and you may have to deal with something unexpected. While it is therefore important to keep in mind the information and training you have been given, you may also have to call upon your own good sense, thoughtfulness, and caution to deal appropriately with what you face. It also bears repeating that if there is someone to ask for help or explanation, do so—training volunteers and understanding their predicaments is very much part of a supervisor's role. But learning how to deal with uncomfortable situations is probably going to be part of your own education as a volunteer.

It is almost inevitable that you will face some problems or concerns either before you become a volunteer or while volunteering. Whether this is a question of changing your schedule, or an unavoidable absence, or a specific issue with which you are faced while you are working, the most important thing is to *communicate*. Speak with your supervisor to discuss the issue and find a way to resolve it. The organizations that depend on volunteers and the supervisors who work with volunteers want to make the volunteer experience a good one; it is in their best interest to engage their volunteers successfully, to keep them motivated and involved. If you have a problem, they want—and need—to hear about it.

OBSTACLES TO VOLUNTEERING

While it is my goal to encourage young people to find meaningful ways to volunteer, I also recognize that there are obstacles that may make it more difficult to find ways to do so. But as with so many seeming obstacles in life, when one looks closely at them, analyzes what the obstacle actually is, and thinks about how to overcome it, the obstacle disappears. If you feel you are confronting obstacles to volunteering, take a closer look.

FINDING THE TIME TO VOLUNTEER

Everyone has busy schedules these days, particularly teenagers. Between school, homework, sports, and other extracurricular activities, it sometimes seems like there isn't even time for recreation or relaxation. So how does one find time for a volunteer job?

If committing to a regular ongoing schedule is not something you feel you can fit into your busy life, aim for one-day opportunities. Carve out that time in your schedule and plan for it. Sign up with a friend or group of friends to help you stick to your plan, and hopefully you will find that the experience not only makes you feel good about doing good, but also you'll enjoy the day—and share the good feeling—with friends.

If you *do* want to make the commitment to a longer-term opportunity, it often turns out that by scheduling it thoughtfully into your week, you'll find you can make it happen. Just make sure you can honor the time commitment—that you take into consideration the other demands on your time and be sure you can make it all work.

THE COMPLEXITIES OF FINDING AND APPLYING FOR A VOLUNTEER PLACEMENT

Some young people are daunted by the prospect of finding a volunteer opportunity that interests them, and others are intimidated by the sometimes complex process of applying once they've identified an area of interest. Hopefully this book will help guide prospective volunteers through the process and offer suggestions for further information. Sam, one young volunteer, had a perceptive thought about the process of becoming a volunteer that organizations and agencies that use volunteers should definitely keep in mind when trying to recruit volunteers: "When you don't have an easy way to volunteer, it's just too easy *not* to volunteer."

THE HIDDEN COST OF VOLUNTEERING

When money is tight, it may be hard to find time to volunteer because that time may be able to be filled by a paying job. But for young teens and, in this economy, people of any age, finding a paying job can be difficult. There's still the question of whether to take a volunteer job when it may be possible to find a job and earn money during that time. As one young man commented, "Why would I give my time away when I can earn something?" Indeed, another young man put it even more directly: "If I'm poor, why would I want to help other people?"

This last question, I hope, was answered in the first chapter, but there is no question that there can be hidden costs to volunteering. Unless you can walk to your volunteer job, getting there may require travel expenses; even if you get a ride to your volunteer job, *someone* is paying for the gas being used. In addition, if you will be working many hours, will you have to pay for a snack or meal? Occasionally a volunteer must purchase a uniform, for example, a t-shirt or jacket. Thus, it is important to consider what costs would be involved in being a volunteer and then decide (and perhaps discuss with your parents) whether you can afford to do it.

It is rare, but there are occasionally programs that can help pay for carfare or offer a meal subsidy for volunteers. If the cost of volunteering would prevent you from participating in an opportunity you feel strongly about pursuing, speak up; ask your guidance counselor or teacher if they know of any subsidies. Similarly, ask the volunteer program or research community organizations that might offer support for such an endeavor. As with many things, you won't know if you don't ask.

MISUNDERSTANDINGS

"Only rich white girls volunteer."

I actually heard this twice, as a question, from young people I interviewed. In my own experience running a program for high school
volunteers in New York City, I saw that this was very much *not* the
case. I had volunteers from inner-city public high schools, independent
schools, and parochial and other religious schools. I had students who
identified at every point on the gender scale. I had students from widely
diverse cultures, religions, backgrounds, and nationalities, and students
who came from every level of the socioeconomic stratum. This diversity
may be a function of being in a large multicultural city like New York,
but these volunteers were certainly *not* only rich white girls.

I recently spoke with someone who runs a leadership institute for
high school students, who, as part of the program, help develop lessons
for service programs in local schools. The service program curricula deal
with topics that city children face, notably such issues as homelessness
and pollution. One of the important things these students learn is that
service is a two-way street. For instance, homeless students who participated in the homelessness module found themselves empowered through
the experience, learning that while they were performing service, they
were getting something from it, too. Programs like that, which include
volunteers from every segment of society, can be great equalizers.

"You have to be an expert to volunteer."

While some volunteers *are* experts before they volunteer, most people
are not. One of the greatest opportunities in being a volunteer is to
become good at something. Volunteers can be even more valuable when
they have no prior experience but are eager to learn and help do whatever they can. Of course, an expert who volunteers their expertise to an
organization that *needs* that special skill can be extraordinarily useful.
For example, if you are a technical wizard with computers, an organization might greatly appreciate your help setting up a new computer

system or teaching someone to use it. But one thing that is not generally of benefit to an organization is a volunteer who *only* wants to offer the skill in which they excel, if it's not one that's particularly needed. So, if you're a computer wizard but the organization *really* needs someone to organize sing-alongs, that might be where you can be most useful. Adaptability is a valuable asset in a volunteer.

"Some people might hesitate to volunteer," Hannah K. told me.

They don't exactly know what it means to volunteer or are afraid of not knowing what they're supposed to do. I think that's what intimidates people the most; they think, "I don't know what to do" or "I don't know how this works, or where I'm supposed to go." My advice for that is, don't be afraid to reach out to people.

"Volunteering is just a job with no pay. Why should I do that?"

I hope chapter 1 answered this question. But to reiterate the major points, volunteering is more than just a job with no pay. It is an opportunity to serve your community, country, and world; it is a chance to learn, experience a wider sphere, meet people you might not otherwise meet, and give yourself to something larger than you. It is spiritually, psychologically, and emotionally fulfilling *because* you are not getting paid to do it. As Bella said to me, based on her experience, "Everyone loves volunteers. There are no negatives. You won't lose from volunteering. Try it: You'll feel good as you do good."

CHAPTER SIX

FINDING YOUR AREA OF INTEREST AS A PROSPECTIVE VOLUNTEER

Volunteers enrich our lives every day with their generosity and compassion.
—Bill Clinton, forty-second president of the United States[1]

This list is intended to get you thinking about areas beyond those already mentioned in this book in which you might like to volunteer. Some may be already part of a locally run program in your community or school, some may give you an idea about starting a special interest club at your school, and some may make you think of similar areas you would like to pursue. Use this list as a guide for further research.

WORK AS AN USHER AT A BENEFIT CONCERT

Working at a benefit concert can be a great way to support an organization and—if you're lucky—hear music you enjoy. There may be opportunities to help out as an usher, taking tickets, giving out wristbands, directing people to their seats, or helping in the venue office. If you see a poster or ad announcing a local benefit concert raising money for a charitable organization, try getting in touch and offering your services.

START A BLOG FOR A CAUSE YOU CARE ABOUT

Writing and posting on a blog in support of a cause you believe in can be a great way for a young person to volunteer their time and know-how. Many organizations list that as an opportunity on their websites.

VOLUNTEER FOR A BLOOD DRIVE (EVEN IF YOU ARE TOO YOUNG TO DONATE BLOOD)

There are many local drives encouraging people to donate blood; some are scheduled, annual appeals, and some are in response to a specific need: Blood may be in critical supply during certain seasons or if there has been an emergency. Although blood donation is usually limited to those sixteen years of age and older, there are other ways young people can help. Kris helped organize a blood drive at her school, but when she learned it was going to be cancelled because of unexpected renovation in the school auditorium, she contacted the blood center and worked with them to get a Bloodmobile (mobile blood donation unit) to park outside her school and helped ensure that the event ran smoothly, including arranging to get the necessary permissions, alerting teachers to the changes, and putting up flyers about the event.

BECOME A CONVERSATION PARTNER

For someone for whom English is not a native language, becoming comfortable speaking English takes more than learning grammar or vocabulary. You can help someone become more comfortable speaking by simply making conversation. Some schools, hospitals, and community centers offer the opportunity to be a "conversation partner" and will pair you up with a nonnative English speaker for regular half-hour or one-hour time slots. There's no guidance or limits on what the conversation can be about—you and your partner can talk about anything you like, and the more you do it, the more you can get to know and help another person in a relaxed way.

KNIT OR CROCHET BLANKETS OR NEWBORN CAPS FOR NEEDY BABIES

If knitting or crocheting is something you already like to do or would like to learn to do, making blankets or caps for newborns is a good way to practice something you enjoy and do good while doing it. This can be a good activity to build a club around or do on your own. Inquire at a local craft or knitting store, or a local hospital, about whether they already have such a program or if you can start one for them.

PICK UP TRASH AND RECYCLABLES ALONG THE HIGHWAY OR IN A PARK AND DISPOSE OF THEM APPROPRIATELY

Another great group activity is to organize a bunch of friends—adults welcome—to spend a few hours on a Sunday or holiday cleaning up the trash and recyclables that end up scattered along roadways and throughout parks. This is something that can be done without being formalized through an organization—it's just good for the community.

READ ALOUD TO SOMEONE WHO IS BLIND OR HAS VISUAL IMPAIRMENTS

Like to read? Many people do, but for someone who is blind or has visual impairments, it may not be something they can enjoy; however, many people enjoy—and even depend on—having someone read aloud to them. Ask a local senior center, nursing home, or hospital if they can connect you with someone who would value your time and willingness to read. Whether it's reading the newspaper or magazines, a book, stories, or even the Bible, this can be a wonderful way to forge a genuine relationship based on a mutual love of the written word.

COACH A YOUTH SPORTS TEAM

Love basketball? Soccer? Some other sport? If you know the rules of the sport, and even if you are not an elite athlete, you can put your energy, knowledge, and enthusiasm to good use coaching a local youth sports team.

PLAY MUSIC OR SING IN A NURSING HOME OR HOSPITAL

Have a musical talent? As Evan C. discovered, playing music or singing can provide entertainment and distraction for patients, and it is a great way to become better and more confident in your performance skills. Contact local nursing homes or hospitals to find out how you might do this.

HELP CLEAR LITTER AND REMOVE WEEDS FROM A CEMETERY

Some houses of worship have affiliated cemeteries, and many organize annual spring cleanup days when congregants help clear litter, remove weeds, and plant flowers around graves. This is a good way to join with friends in an outdoor activity that has value for your community and honors those who have died.

MAKE BIRTHDAY OR HOLIDAY CARDS FOR DISTRIBUTION AT A HOSPITAL OR HOMELESS SHELTER

This is a good activity to do with friends and even possibly make the theme of a party or get-together. Being a hospitalized patient or someone living in a homeless shelter can be lonely and isolating, but receiving a cheerful greeting card for a holiday or birthday—even from someone they've never met—can help brighten a person's spirits. Contact the volunteer department of a local hospital or a shelter's office to find out if and how you can deliver such cards and get your friends and arts and crafts materials together, and enjoy the opportunity as a group.

PREPARE NECESSITIES KITS (SOAP, TOOTHBRUSH, TOOTHPASTE, SHAMPOO, ETC.) TO BE DISTRIBUTED AFTER A DISASTER

This is another worthwhile activity that can be done alone, with your family, or in a group. If your school, community center, club, or congregation is already organized to do this, it's easy to participate. If not, identify a distribution center (a good place to start is by contacting the Red Cross) and find out what they need and where you can deliver it. If there isn't already a fund to purchase supplies, see if you can raise the money necessary to buy quantities of travel/sample-size toiletries, or solicit donations of those items from a neighborhood pharmacy or supermarket. Make up the kits in plastic or paper bags and deliver them to the distribution center to be handed out to those in need.

TRAIN WITH YOUR PET TO BECOME CERTIFIED AS A "PET-ASSISTED THERAPY" TEAM

Many hospitals and nursing homes are now welcoming "pet-assisted therapy" teams, specially trained and certified animals and owners who visit patients and residents to offer comfort, affection, and a friendly visit. Therapy pets are also being used in schools and libraries as nonjudgmental listeners for children who may need practice reading aloud. Animals must be calm, friendly, and well-trained in basic commands, and both animal and human companion must complete and be certified by a recognized training program.

PLAY CHESS WITH SENIORS IN A SENIOR CENTER OR TEACH CHESS TO KIDS AT AN AFTER-SCHOOL PROGRAM

If chess is your thing, volunteering to play or teach chess is a wonderful way to engage with someone, young or old. As with music, playing chess not only provides enjoyment for the person with whom you play, but also helps you improve your own skills. Similarly, teaching a skill is always an excellent way to better understand and enhance your own abilities.

There are many different ways for volunteers to get involved in their community.

HELP WITH OFFICE WORK IN THE HEADQUARTERS OF A CAUSE YOU SUPPORT

Whether it's a political organization, religious organization, or nonprofit supporting medical issues, homelessness, the environment, or any number of other causes, it's almost a given that there is always a need for more people to help. If you're good at organization and can file paperwork, answer phones, and sort or prepare materials, working in the office of a cause you believe in can introduce you to other like-minded individuals and offer you the chance to gain experience working in an office environment, which could be invaluable in the future.

VOLUNTEER FOR A POLITICAL CANDIDATE WHOSE PLATFORM YOU ADMIRE

Political campaigns rely on volunteers to staff offices, knock on doors, help organize rallies, and otherwise promote the message of the campaign. Whether it's a local, statewide, or national campaign, inquire at the closest campaign headquarters as to how you might best be able to help. It's best to carefully learn about and consider the policies and promises of the campaign to ensure that you are working for someone you generally support—and it's a wonderful way to become more politically aware and active, even if you are not yet old enough to vote.

WALK DOGS (OR PLAY WITH CATS) AT AN ANIMAL SHELTER

Most animal shelters rely on volunteers to help socialize and exercise the animals in their care; some volunteers also help clean cages and play areas or help in the office. Contact local shelters to find out what the expectations are. If you've always dreamed of having a pet but have not been able to have your own, volunteering for a shelter is a great way to enjoy the pleasure of interacting with animals and know you're giving them the love and attention they deserve.

PARTICIPATE IN A BUTTERFLY (OR HONEYBEE) CENSUS

This can be an exciting way to be involved in an important environmental cause. The number of butterflies and honeybees can be an important measure of the health of the environment, and at times volunteers are needed to participate in censuses—actually counting the number of butterflies or honeybees in a particular area. Search online for "butterfly census volunteer" or "honeybee census volunteer" to learn if there is any such opportunity near you.

TAKE PHOTOGRAPHS FOR YOUR LOCAL SCHOOL, HOUSE OF WORSHIP, OR SENIOR CENTER

As Jeremy found out, his synagogue was happy to use his photographs to illustrate their newsletters and flyers. If photography is your interest and you have some skill in taking good pictures, offer to take pictures for your school or congregation, or at a local senior center. As with music, chess, and other talents, it's a great way to gain more experience and polish your skills.

HELP OUT AT A LOCAL NURSERY SCHOOL OR CHILD CARE CENTER

If you enjoy being with kids, there are often opportunities for teens to help at local child care or nursery school sites. It helps—but isn't necessarily a requirement—to have babysitting experience, whether with your own siblings or neighborhood children.

TUTOR ELEMENTARY SCHOOL STUDENTS IN A SUBJECT AT WHICH YOU EXCEL

Many elementary schools are happy to have older students as volunteer tutors, especially for reading and math. There may be organized tutoring programs you can join or you may be able to make a place for yourself as an individual tutor by inquiring at a local school. Another great way to interact with little kids is to read stories; it boosts children's literacy abilities and is a friendly and comforting interaction that is immensely enjoyable to both reader and listener. Libraries, hospitals, and homeless shelters may be glad to have teen volunteer readers.

ASSIST AT A COMMUNITY PLAYGROUND SUMMER CAMP

Many neighborhood playgrounds offer free or low-cost summer day camp activities and may be glad to have teen volunteers to assist in the activities. Announcements of camper enrollment may be posted in community listservs, on flyers at supermarkets or shops, or at the playground. Participating in an opportunity like this, even if it is in a relatively informal capacity, can help you gain experience and skills you can build on in the future.

ORGANIZE AN ARTS AND CRAFTS PROGRAM FOR A LOCAL CHILD CARE CENTER, SENIOR CENTER, OR NURSING HOME

If you enjoy crafts and creativity, you may be able to put that creativity to good use volunteering those skills at a child care center or senior residence. As Hannah K. found, when she volunteered her services at a local school for children with special needs, arts and crafts activities were a great way to engage with them.

HELP BRING MEALS TO ISOLATED SENIORS

Whether through a branch of Meals on Wheels, a local house of worship, or some other community organization, many isolated seniors rely on these services not only for the important nutrition they provide, but also the companionship they receive from those who deliver the meals. Sometimes the meal delivery volunteer is the only person they get to see for days, so those few minutes of time when the meals are brought can be a rare and important social interaction and occasionally develop into warm and affectionate friendships. Check out local organizations that offer this service and inquire about opportunities for teen volunteers. It can be immensely rewarding to make such a difference in the life of an older, lonely person.

PART III

WHAT'S NEXT

CHAPTER SEVEN

MAKING THE MOST OF YOUR VOLUNTEERING

I hope that the experience of volunteering is rewarding for you by itself. Nevertheless, consider the ways your volunteer experience can enhance other parts of your life.

WRITING ABOUT YOUR VOLUNTEER EXPERIENCE

I suggested earlier that you keep notes while you volunteer. They can be not only a source of information while you work or a reminder of things you want to know more about, but also a valuable tool for writing about your experience. Whether writing about your volunteer experience is a class requirement, a topic you choose to use for an assignment, or part of a personal journal, it can also become a valuable essay for a college or scholarship application.

When writing an essay about your volunteer experience, especially if it is for a college or scholarship application, make sure you know any specific requirements, for example, the deadline for submission, the number of words it should be, the expected format, or how to submit the essay electronically. In your essay, make sure you include an explanation of the mission of the organization, as well as a description of the area or areas in which the organization works, whom it serves, and how the organization addresses the needs of the people it serves. Describe what your role as a volunteer was, what your specific responsibilities were, and how many hours/days/months you worked there. Include narrative about what you learned and how you felt about what you did and the people you served, as well as how you grew into your role as a volunteer.

An important aspect to describe is what impact your volunteer experience had on your personal growth. Be careful not to exaggerate your role or accomplishments, and avoid clichés. It can be valuable to include negative, as well as positive, experiences, as long as you explain how they were meaningful to you and what you learned from them. Try to make your narrative colorful and lively, yet respectful of the people you served and the organization's work. Express clearly and thoughtfully how the experience was personally meaningful and how it may fit into your future goals, whether academic or career. And as with all good writing, make sure it is well organized, with a structured beginning, middle, and end.

Consider whether there are other places where your written description of your volunteer experience might appear. You may be able to have it published in your school newspaper or even a community newspaper. You might be able to place it on a blog, whether your own or that of the organization itself; many organization websites include a blog, and posting one from a young volunteer about their experience may be something they would be happy to include.

BECOMING A MENTOR OR SUPERVISOR

When you have had a great experience as a volunteer and proven to yourself—and your supervisor or volunteer director—that you are confident in your abilities, know what to do, can use your initiative, and are good at explaining to someone else what your responsibilities are and how to fulfill them, you are probably a good candidate to mentor new or less experienced volunteers. You may be called on to do that without having to suggest it yourself; many organizations routinely ask experienced volunteers to mentor new ones, whether it is just by taking them around the first day and "showing them the ropes" or a more formalized mentoring program, with guidelines as to what you would be expected to cover when you mentor a new volunteer. If you haven't been asked to mentor anyone but think you would like to do it and feel capable of doing so, ask the volunteer director or your immediate supervisor whether there might be a chance for you to mentor new volunteers. Taking the initiative in suggesting this is a good way to demonstrate to them that you take your role seriously and are interested in growing it further.

One of the surest signs that you are a successful volunteer is if you are asked whether you are interested in supervising volunteers. This will probably not happen until you are in your late teens and perhaps not even until you graduate from high school, but it can be an excellent way to transition from volunteerism into a paid position.

Edelysa, who is now in college and hopes to become a social worker, began working as a volunteer at a nursing home when she was a junior in high school. "My high school required two hundred hours of volunteering in order to graduate," she remembered.

> It was intimidating when I first started, but the volunteer who showed me around really spent time explaining things to me. And it turned out that once I got my feet wet, I started really getting into it, and it became fun and changed my whole perspective. After that, I spent more time working there than I was required to do, because I really enjoyed it so much, and I felt that I was learning a lot that would help me when I started my career. Then, at the end of my senior year of high school, when I was finishing my time as a volunteer, the volunteer director at the nursing home asked me whether I might like to be a supervisor for the summer program, when they get a new group of high school volunteers to help the residents. I'm a junior in college now, and I've been a supervisor here for about two and a half years. I love it!

BUILDING YOUR RESUME

Your volunteer experience can have an invaluable impact on the quality of your resume, whether for college or job applications. Volunteer experience demonstrates a commitment to community, service, and exploring areas of personal interest. It gives you an opportunity to list skills and knowledge gained through your volunteer experience and can illustrate an enhanced focus on a particular educational or career path. If you are applying for a job or an academic course of study in an area related to that in which you volunteered, make sure the way you list your volunteer experience demonstrates how it relates to that path; for instance, if you are hoping to go to medical school, your experience as a hospital or laboratory volunteer is certainly relevant to that goal. If you are interested in pursuing a career in public service, having volunteered on a political campaign would align well with that goal. Thinking of becoming a teacher? Your work as a volunteer tutor in a homeless shelter would tie in well with that.

On the other hand, there is value in listing volunteer service that is in a different area than what you hope to pursue, whether academic or job. Nonrelated volunteer service demonstrates a well-rounded, open-minded willingness to explore different areas of interest, as well as acquire skills outside your primary interests.

Your resume should list your volunteer activities under such a heading as "Volunteer Experience" or "Related Experience" if it pertains to an area of academic or career focus. It should name the organization, indicate the time span when you were a volunteer and the area in which you worked, and briefly describe your responsibilities and achievements. Use active rather than passive descriptions of what you did.

EXAMPLE OF HOW TO LIST VOLUNTEER EXPERIENCE ON A RESUME

Central City Hospital, Centralville, New York
Volunteer, General Medicine Unit, September 2018–June 2019

Assisted unit clerk at front desk with answering phones, filing, and admitting patients; visited and engaged patients in conversation; distributed meal trays, water, and magazines; assisted patients with menu selection. From April to June, 2019, mentored new teen volunteers in the unit, in addition to the aforementioned activities.

Central City Animal Shelter, Centralville, New York
Volunteer, September 2018–June 2019

Welcomed prospective pet adopters at the reception desk; processed adoption paperwork; cleaned kennel areas; walked and exercised dogs. Designed an Adopt-a-Pet-Day flyer and created a new brochure for prospective adopters.

If you had a good relationship with your supervisor or someone else who can speak well of your work as a volunteer, ask if you can list them as a reference on your resume. Keep in mind that they will most likely be honest and candid about you, so be thoughtful about who you approach for a reference. A supervisor with whom you established a good rapport can be an invaluable reference and, with luck, a good mentor in years to come.

CHAPTER EIGHT

CONTINUING TO MAKE A DIFFERENCE

As I hope you already recognize, being a volunteer is an important part of communal life; giving your time and energy to help those in need strengthens our communities and is a major ingredient in the concept of "healing the world." Once that you've had a successful volunteer experience, how can you expand on it to continue making a difference?

RECRUIT OTHER VOLUNTEERS

Organizations almost always need new volunteers; it is rare for an organization to have more prospective volunteers than they can use. Assuming that you enjoyed your volunteer experience and feel a continuing connection to the organization and the service it provides, one of the best ways you can continue to benefit it is by helping to recruit other volunteers to work there. There are many ways in which you can do that.

TALK TO YOUR FRIENDS AND CLASSMATES

Whether by informally talking up your experience or volunteering to make a presentation about it at an assembly, club meeting, or other gathering, letting people know about what you did and how you feel about it can be a strong motivator for others. Let your friends know how much you enjoyed it, what you did, how people reacted to you, what you learned, and how it made you feel. If you are going to make a more formal presentation, *be prepared*. Write notes; organize what you would like to say; and know how to describe the work of the organization, the good it does, and the requirements and expectations for volunteers. Decide whether you would be more effective writing out your entire speech or if you are able to communicate effectively relying only on bullet points or notes. And it is always a good idea to *rehearse your presentation*, either aloud to yourself in your own room or in front of an easy audience, like your family or a friend. Get comfortable conveying the information and your enthusiasm through practice.

BE AN AMBASSADOR FOR VOLUNTEERISM

Be willing to "step up to the plate" for any opportunity that may arise to talk about volunteerism and, in particular, volunteering at the organization where you worked. Some schools hold job fairs, where organizations can offer information about their volunteer programs and recruit for volunteers. If your school does this, see whether you can participate as a spokesperson for your organization. It's also a good idea to stay in touch with the volunteer office at the organization where you worked; let them know that you would be happy to talk with prospective volunteers about your experience or participate in any volunteer recruitment activities they may hold.

WRITE ABOUT YOUR EXPERIENCE FOR THE SCHOOL NEWSPAPER, A BLOG, OR YOUR COMMUNITY PAPER

Whether it's a short column or a more extended report, an engaging narrative about your volunteer experience, including how to get in touch with the organization for more information or an application, can help motivate prospective volunteers. You might ask the volunteer director or your supervisor if they are able to use such a personal account as a recruitment tool.

BE A FUNDRAISER FOR THE CAUSE

If you no longer have the time to volunteer or would like to use your volunteer hours elsewhere but still support the organization with which you were involved, you can continue to help them by raising money to support their work. One way is to offer to distribute brochures or fundraising appeals; keep in mind, however, that if you want to distribute them at school or post them in a community space you will probably need permission to do so. If you have family or friends who are able to make monetary gifts to causes they support, suggest that they consider allocating some funds for the organization where you worked. If the organization has a scheduled fundraising event, you might volunteer to assist with it on a one-time basis, even if you are no longer a regular volunteer. Organizations treasure and depend on people who maintain an ongoing relationship with them and are a source of steady support. And even if you are not able to make financial contributions at present, organizations hope that ongoing support like yours may lead you to become a donor at some time in the future when you do have discretionary funds for charitable giving.

CONTINUE TO VOLUNTEER
WHENEVER YOU CAN

There is no question that our lives are busy. Particularly when you are a teenager, your life seems to be filled to overflowing with school, homework, extracurricular activities like sports or music, and, for many young people, jobs—whether paid employment or helping with family chores and taking care of younger siblings. Taking on the added responsibility of volunteering takes a conscious effort and determination to make time in your busy schedule for something you think is important, but as those who do it find, it is possible. It may not *always* be possible, but it's worth doing whenever your life allows you to make time for it.

Whether you go on to volunteer again for an organization where you've already worked or choose other areas in which to volunteer, it is my hope that you will continue to find meaningful ways to volunteer throughout your life, whenever you are able, and continue to encourage and serve as an example for others to become volunteers. Your community, your nation, and the world will be better for it, and you will find your life and your soul enriched by the experience.

CHAPTER NINE
BEYOND VOLUNTEERING

You may find that where your life takes you—or, better put, where you take your life—is rooted in your volunteer experience as a teenager. Elizabeth, who's now in her twenties, volunteered as a high school student with young people with special needs. "I feel like it's the most important thing I've done in my life," she said. "It's why I'm standing here, why I'm the person I am today." And, she added, "You'll feel like a better person when you do it."

Making the most of your volunteer experience has hopefully given you a deeper understanding of the people you helped and the organization for which you worked, as well as greater self-assurance and confidence in your abilities. But for many teenage volunteers, it also ends up influencing what they do in the future.

JIMMY CARTER'S EXAMPLE: A PRESIDENTIAL LEGACY

Jimmy Carter, the thirty-ninth president of the United States, is a living example of the power of volunteerism to inspire. After serving as president from 1977 to 1981, President Carter devoted himself to advancing the cause of social justice, human rights, and alleviating the suffering of people throughout the world by establishing a nongovernmental organization, the Carter Center. In March 1984, he joined former First Lady Rosalyn Carter in volunteering with Habitat for Humanity to build affordable housing for those in need. Since that time, through the Carter

---

Work Project, he and Mrs. Carter have volunteered for one week each year to continue this effort. President and Mrs. Carter have worked alongside more than one hundred thousand volunteers in fourteen countries to build, renovate, and repair more than four thousand homes.[1] The vibrant and committed example they have set, continuing even this year, as President Carter approached his ninety-fifth birthday, continues to inspire and motivate thousands of volunteers worldwide. Along with his decades-long dedication to finding peaceful solutions to international conflict, for which he won the Nobel Peace Prize in 2002, President Carter's example of committed volunteerism will surely stand as one of his greatest legacies.

A recent study by Volunteer Service Overseas[2] identified three areas in which volunteer involvement influenced future activities: Volunteering increases levels of social action; volunteering often changes career direction; and volunteers experience an increase in self-awareness and cultural awareness. How might these changes affect you beyond your volunteer experience?

Of the volunteers included in the study, more than three-quarters reported changes in the level of their social action after volunteering. Of these, more than eight out of ten attributed these changes to their experience as volunteers. Not surprisingly, an increase in volunteers' cultural awareness and self-awareness developed through their volunteer experience inspired them to attempt to positively influence others, for example, by challenging negative stereotypes and behavior. How might this be something you can do? It might be something as simple as not letting a culturally insensitive remark pass unchallenged during a conversation with classmates or peers. Or, extending your influence beyond your immediate circle, you might give a presentation at school, write a blog about your experience, join a group involved in advocacy through your school or community, or even join efforts to influence government, for instance, by writing letters or participating in a lobbying activity. These are ways you can carry the benefits of your volunteer experience beyond the act of volunteering itself.

The same study also showed that volunteering often leads to heightened personal drive or motivation, which, for young volunteers, often helps them to expand or solidify their thoughts about a future career. At times, as mentioned earlier, your experience as a volunteer might influence or change what you previously thought you wanted to do as a career or the academic path you hoped to take. Similarly, a mentor, volunteer leader, or supervisor who you admire might be an influence on you or even be someone you choose to model. Having a successful role model can lead to increased self-confidence, as well as a more determined and clearly defined academic or career path.

With the increased confidence and self-assurance a successful volunteer experience can give you, you may find that you also gain a calmer, more thoughtful approach to life after volunteering, in addition to a greater sense of empathy and understanding for others. Cheyenne, who volunteered with a therapeutic riding program, had some thoughtful suggestions: "Initially, in any volunteer experience, one should think, 'Can I contribute to this environment? Can I impact the constituents? And, what impact will it have not only on their lives, but on my life?'" Self-confidence, resilience, and adaptability are three areas in which many successful volunteers find personal growth and are valuable tools to help with the many stresses of the teen years and beyond.

Another way to take what you learn from volunteering beyond the experience itself and apply it productively later in life is highlighted in a piece written by Dr. John M. Anderson, former president of Alfred State College of the State University of New York. In it, Dr. Anderson discusses not only how volunteering is vitally important and an excellent way to learn about why a societal problem exists and what one can do about it, but also, of equal importance, that volunteering is often the first step to getting more involved in civic engagement. According to Dr. Anderson, it is necessary to learn to ask the difficult questions about societal problems, explore the root causes of a given circumstance, and then find and implement solutions through civic engagement.[3]

You can build on your volunteer experience by looking more closely at problems within your own community, asking why things are the way they are and thinking about—and working to develop—the means to solve them. Going beyond that, you can then begin to look at how those same problems and solutions may occur on a larger scale elsewhere in the world and work to address them. I do not mean to imply that this is something you, as an individual, will do alone, but your volunteer experience can—and hopefully will—encourage you to look beyond yourself and find ways to engage with others to address important societal problems. Global issues of hunger, abuse, poverty, medical care, education, and the environment will require tremendous amounts of civic engagement to solve. Those people, like you, who have looked at these issues firsthand, through volunteer experience, can be integral in helping to ask the questions, seek the answers, and find ways to implement solutions to improve lives and the life of our planet in years to come.

NOTES

YOU ARE NOT ALONE

1. "Volunteer," *Merriam-Webster Dictionary* (Springfield, MA: Merriam-Webster, 1997), 822.
2. "Volunteer," *Oxford Living Dictionaries*, 2018, https://en.oxforddiction aries.com/definition/volunteer (accessed January 29, 2020).
3. "Proclamation 4288, April 20, 1974, National Volunteer Week, 1974," *GovInfo*, https://www.govinfo.gov/content/pkg/STATUTE-88 /pdf/STATUTE-88-Pg2476.pdf (accessed January 29, 2020).
4. "Youth Helping America: The Role of Social Institutions in Teen Volunteering," *Corporation for National and Community Service*, November, 2005, www.nationalservice.gov/pdf/05_1130_LSA_YHA_ SI_factsheet.pdf (accessed January 29, 2020).

CHAPTER ONE: WHY VOLUNTEER?

1. From President Bill Clinton's Proclamation for National Volunteer Week, 1996, "Presidential Documents: Proclamation 6885 of April 17, 1996, National Volunteer Week, 1996," *GovInfo*, https://www.govinfo .gov/content/pkg/FR-1996-04-19/pdf/96-9912.pdf (accessed January 29, 2020).
2. "DoSomething.org Index on Young People and Volunteering," *Dosomething.org*, 2012, https://www.dosomething.org/sites/default/files /blog/2012-Web-Singleview_0.pdf (accessed January 29, 2020).
3. "Volunteering as Pathway to Employment," *Corporation for National and Community Service*, https://www.nationalservice.gov/sites/default/files /upload/employment_research_report.pdf (accessed January 29, 2020).
4. "DoSomething.org Index on Young People and Volunteering."

CHAPTER TWO:
GETTING STARTED AS A VOLUNTEER

1. From Ronald Reagan's Proclamation for National Volunteer Week, 1987, "Proclamation 5639—National Volunteer Week, 1987: Our Constitutional Heritage," *Ronald Reagan Presidential Library and Museum*, https://www.reaganlibrary.gov/research/speeches/0426 87a (accessed January 28, 2020).
2. Sarah D. Sparks, "Volunteerism Declined among Young People, Yet Interest in Doing Good Reached a High Point," *Education Week*, July 17, 2018, https://www.edweek.org/ew/articles/2018/07/18/volunteerism -declined-among-young-people.html (accessed January 28, 2020).
3. "Charity," *Oxford Dictionaries*, https://en.oxforddictionaries.com/defi nition/charity (accessed January 28, 2020).
4. President Bill Clinton, Proclamation for National Volunteer Week, 1997, "Proclamation 6986 of April 11, 1997, National Service and Volunteer Week, 1997," *GovInfo*, https://www.govinfo.gov/content /pkg/FR1997-04-15/pdf/97-9914.pdf (accessed January 28, 2020).

CHAPTER THREE:
WHAT MAKES A SUCCESSFUL VOLUNTEER?

1. From President George W. Bush's Proclamation for National Volunteer Week, 2001, "National Volunteer Week, 2001, by the President of the United States of America: A Proclamation," *White House*, https://georgew bush-whitehouse.archives.gov/news/releases/2001/04/20010417.html (accessed January 28, 2020).

CHAPTER FOUR:
WHAT YOU LEARN AS A VOLUNTEER

1. From President George W. Bush's Proclamation for National Volunteer Week, 2004, "Proclamation 7773—National Volunteer Week, 2004," *GovInfo*, https://www.govinfo.gov/content/pkg/WCPD-2004-04-26/ pdf/WCPD-2004-04-26-Pg622.pdf (accessed January 28,2020).

CHAPTER FIVE: VOLUNTEER CHALLENGES

1. From President Barack Obama's Proclamation for National Volunteer Week, 2009, "Presidential Proclamation—National Volunteer Week," *White House*, https://obamawhitehouse.archives.gov/the-press-office /2011/04/07/presidential-proclamation-national-volunteer-week (accessed January 28, 2020).

CHAPTER SIX: FINDING YOUR AREA OF INTEREST AS A PROSPECTIVE VOLUNTEER

1. From President Bill Clinton's Proclamation for National Volunteer Week, 1998, "Proclamation 7085 of April 21, 1998, National Volunteer Week, 1998," *GovInfo*, https://govinfo.gov/content/pkg/FR-1998-04 -23/pdf/98-11024.pdf (accessed January 28, 2020).

CHAPTER NINE: BEYOND VOLUNTEERING

1. "Carter Work Project," *Habitat for Humanity*, https://www.habitat .org/volunteer/build-events/carter-work-project (accessed January 28, 2020).
2. Janet Clark and Simon Lewis, "Impact Beyond Volunteering," *Voluntary Service Overseas*, December 2016, https://www.vsointernational.org /sites/default/files/VSO_ImpactBeyondVolunteering_MainReport_ web.pdf (accessed January 28, 2020).
3. John M. Anderson, "Beyond Volunteering: Civic Engagement in Action," *Huffington Post*, November 24, 2012, https://www.huffpost .com/entry/beyond-volunteering-civic_b_1904635 (accessed January 28, 2020).

SELECTED
RESOURCES

American Cancer Society
250 Williams Street NW
Atlanta, GA 30303
https://www.cancer.org/involved/volunteer.html
Teens can help support cancer patients and survivors through participating in community events.

American Lung Association
55 W. Wacker Drive, Suite 1150
Chicago, IL 60601
https://www.lung.org/get-involved/volunteer/
Teens can create community projects to promote tobacco-free environments and increase awareness about the realities of tobacco use.

American Red Cross
431 18th Street NW
Washington, DC 20006
https://www.redcross.org/volunteer/volunteer-opportunities.html
The American Red Cross mobilizes volunteers to alleviate suffering in the face of emergencies. Twenty-five percent of Red Cross volunteers are twenty-four years old or younger. Teens can find ways to help through school clubs, youth councils, and other opportunities.

Amnesty International USA
5 Penn Plaza, 16th Floor
New York, NY 10001
https://www.amnestyusa.org/take-action/volunteer/
Amnesty International is an international grassroots movement dedicated
to protecting human rights. Join or learn how to establish a student group.

Best Buddies International, Inc.
100 SE 2nd Street, #2200
Miami, FL 33131
https://www.bestbuddies.org/
Working to end the social, physical, and economic isolation of people
with intellectual and developmental disabilities, volunteers can join an
established chapter or start one at school to help with events, fundraising activities, and recreational opportunities.

Boy Scouts of America
National Service Center
PO Box 152079
Irving, TX 75015
https://www.scouting.org/
Boy Scouts help young people appreciate and respond to the needs of
others through engagement in community service.

Congressional Award
PO Box 77440
Washington, DC 20002
http://congressionalaward.org/about/
The Congressional Award is awarded to young Americans who set and
meet personal goals in four areas: volunteer public service, personal
development, physical fitness, and expedition/exploration. There is no
minimum grade point average requirement. This program can accom-
modate young people with special needs or disabilities who are willing
to take the challenge.

Delivering Good
266 West 37th Street, 22nd Floor
New York, NY 10018
https://www.delivering-good.org/community-partners/volunteering
  -opportunities/
Delivering Good partners with community organizations to deliver donated goods to people in crisis.

DoSomething.org
19 West 21st Street, 8th Floor
New York, NY 10010
https://www.DoSomething.org/us
DoSomething.org mobilizes young people to participate in volunteer, social change, or civic action campaigns.

Earth Force
PO Box 1228
Denver, CO 80201
https://earthforce.org/
Earth Force partners with school districts and environmental organizations to engage students in confronting environmental challenges by incorporating civic experiences into STEM and environmental education. The program helps students become active participants in their communities by conducting research, building strong community partnerships, and making decisions as a democratic group.

EXCEL Clubs
National Exchange Club
3050 Central Avenue
Toledo, OH 43606
https://members.nationalexchangeclub.org/content/excel-clubs
EXCEL Clubs are the youth branch of the National Exchange Club, a progressive national service organization. EXCEL Clubs are groups of high school students dedicated to improving their schools, communities, and country through volunteerism.

Family-to-Family
PO Box 255
Hastings-on-Hudson, NY 10706
https://www.family-to-family.org/
A grassroots hunger and poverty relief organization that helps families
find ways to help families struggling with the challenges of poverty.

Generation On (Points of Light)
600 Means Street, Suite 210
Atlanta, GA 30318
https://www.generationon.org/
The youth branch of the Points of Light organization, Generation On
provides programs, tools, and resources to engage teens in service and
volunteering.

Girl Scouts of America
420 Fifth Avenue
New York, NY 10018
https://www.generationon.org/
Girl Scouts participate in community service projects both in groups
and individually.

Global Crossroad
415 West Airport Freeway, Suite 375
Irving, TX 75062
https://www.globalcrossroad.com/best-cheap-summer-volunteer
    -programs-for-high-school-students/
Global Crossroad offers a wide array of safe and affordable volunteer
summer programs for high school students.

Global Youth Action Network
211 East 43rd Street, Suite 905
New York, NY 10017
https://changingthepresent.org/collections/global-youth-action
-network
The Global Youth Action Network (GYAN) links youth organizations in almost two hundred countries to help young people work together to solve the world's problems.

Habitat for Humanity
270 Peachtree Street NW, Suite 1300
Atlanta, GA 30303
https://www.habitat.org/volunteer/near-you/youth-programs
Through Habitat for Humanity, young volunteers can become involved in strengthening their own neighborhoods and communities, and participate in meaningful work with a wide variety of people.

Hugh O'Brian Youth Leadership
31255 Cedar Valley Drive, Suite 327
Westlake Village, CA 91362
https://www.hoby.org/
Hugh O'Brian Youth Leadership (HOBY) is an organization whose mission is to inspire youth to dedicate their lives to leadership, service, and dedication. Students participate in leadership seminars and engage in community service.

Humane Society of the United States
1255 23rd Street NW
Washington, DC 20037
https://www.humanesociety.org/volunteer
The Humane Society website can help you find volunteer opportunities with animal rescue organizations in your area.

Idealist.org
https://www.idealist.org/en/?type=VOLOP
Idealist.org is an online service for job hunters that also helps connect prospective volunteers with organizations.

Key Club (Kiwanis International)
c/o Key Club International
3636 Woodview Trace
Indianapolis, IN 46268
https://www.keyclub.org/
High school student members of Key Club, a youth division of the Kiwanis, perform acts of service in their communities, for example, cleaning up parks, collecting clothing, and organizing food drives. They also learn leadership skills by running meetings; planning projects; and holding elected leadership positions at the club, district, and international levels.

Lion's Heart
19782 MacArthur Boulevard, Suite 310
Irvine, CA 92612
https://lionsheartservice.org/lh2/
Lion's Heart connects teens with nonprofit community service and volunteer opportunities, and helps keep track of volunteer hours online.

National Park Service
1849 C Street NW
Washington, DC 20240
https://www.nps.gov/getinvolved/volunteer.htm
The National Park Service offers a variety of volunteer opportunities for individuals and groups as part of the Volunteers-In-Parks program. Opportunities are available at park locations throughout the United States, including the territories in the Pacific and the Caribbean.

Nature Conservancy
4245 North Fairfax Drive, Suite 100
Arlington, VA 22203
https://www.nature.org/en-us/get-involved/how-to-help/volunteer-and
-attend-events/
The Nature Conservancy works to tackle climate change, protect land
and water, build healthy cities, and provide food and water sustain-
ably. Volunteers work on such projects as monitoring bird populations,
planting trees, and removing invasive plant species.

Organization for Autism Research
2000 N. 14th Street, Suite 300
Arlington, VA 22201
https://researchautism.org/get-involved/volunteer/
Volunteers with the Organization for Autism Research (OAR) can help
with advocacy, education, or fundraising efforts to support people and
families of people with autism.

Pet Partners
345 118th Avenue, SE #200
Bellevue, WA 98005
https://petpartners.org
Pet Partners is a national leader in animal-assisted therapy, activities,
education, and training.

Presidential Volunteer Service Award
c/o Points of Light
600 Means Street NW, Suite 210
Atlanta, GA 30318
https://www.presidentialserviceawards.gov/about
The Presidential Volunteer Service Award recognizes those who have
achieved a required number of hours of service during a twelve-month
time period or cumulative hours during the course of a lifetime.

Project Sunshine
211 E. 43rd Street, #401
New York, NY 10017
https://projectsunshine.org/volunteers/
Project Sunshine works with medical centers throughout the United
States to create cheerful places for pediatric patients and families. School
and community groups, as well as individual volunteers, can help with
their creative and educational projects.

Prudential Spirit of Community Award
1321 Murfreesboro Road, Suite 800
Nashville, TN 37217
https://spirit.prudential.com/
The Prudential Spirit of Community Awards are based exclusively
on volunteer community service. The award honors middle and high
school students for outstanding service to others at the local, state, and
national levels.

Reach Out and Read
89 South Street, Suite 201
Boston, MA 02111
http://www.reachoutandread.org/join-us/volunteer/
Reach Out and Read volunteer readers provide a positive reading experience to children in clinics and medical practices.

Reading Is Fundamental
750 First Street NE, Suite 920
Washington, DC 20002
https://www.rif.org/literacy-network/volunteer/
Reading Is Fundamental (RIF) promotes childhood literacy; RIF volunteers serve as reading mentors in their own community.

Ronald McDonald House (Ronald McDonald House Charities)
110 North Carpenter Street
Chicago, IL 60607
https://www.rmhc.org/volunteer
Ronald McDonald House Charities works to keep families with sick children together and near the medical care they need. Volunteers help with cooking, hosting, listening, and just being there and helping out in any way they can.

Salvation Army
615 Slaters Lane
PO Box 269
Alexandria, VA 22313
https://www.salvationarmy.org/
An international movement, the Salvation Army is an evangelical part of the Christian Church. Teens can volunteer by ringing bells during the holiday season, as well as get involved with fundraising, mentoring, volunteering in shelters, food pantries, and emergency disaster relief.

Sierra Club
1010 Webster Street, Suite 1300
Oakland, CA 94612
https://www.sierraclub.org/volunteer
The Sierra Club offers paid teen travel experiences to camp, learn, and do service projects to help protect and maintain America's great outdoors.

Special Olympics
1133 19th Street NW
Washington, DC 20036
https://www.specialolympics.org/get-involved/volunteer
The Special Olympics provides year-round sports training and athletic competition for children and adults with intellectual disabilities; volunteers help in many capacities throughout the year.

Students against Destructive Decisions
1440 G Street NW
Washington, DC 20005
https://www.sadd.org
The mission of Students against Destructive Decisions (SADD) is to empower young people to successfully confront the risks and pressures that challenge them throughout their daily lives through a network of student-run chapters in schools and communities focused on peer-to-peer education.

Teenlife.com
https://www.teenlife.com/category/volunteer/
Teenlife.com is an online guide to enrichment programs for teens, including thousands of nonprofit organizations in all fifty states that accept teens younger than age eighteen who are interested in everything from working with animals to volunteering at homeless shelters.

TeensGive.org
http://www.teensgive.org/
TeensGive.org is a nonprofit organization designed to provide both in-person and virtual volunteer opportunities for high school students.

Together We Rise
580 W. Lambert Road, #A
Brea, CA 92821
https://www.togetherwerise.org/volunteer-opportunities/
The mission of Together We Rise is to help ease the transitions that foster children experience in the foster care system. Teens can participate in service projects and team-building activities.

UNICEF
3 United Nations Plaza
New York, NY 10017
https://www.unicefusa.org/supporters/volunteers/volunteering-faqs
UNICEF works in 190 countries and territories to save children's lives, defend their rights, and help them fulfill their potential. UNICEF has helped save the lives of more children than any other organization. UNICEF Clubs partner with UNICEF USA to activate local communities by advocating, building community, fundraising, and serving as ambassadors for UNICEF's work.

United Nations Online Volunteering
https://www.onlinevolunteering.org/en
The United Nations offers opportunities for volunteers to work on specific projects online to help promote peace and development throughout the world.

United States Forest Service
Sidney R. Yates Federal Building
201 14th Street, NW
Washington, DC 20024
https://www.fs.fed.us/working-with-us/volunteers
United States Forest Service volunteers help run events and lead projects, participate in Citizen Science projects, help build trails, inventory wildlife and plants, and much more.

United Way/Student United Way
701 N. Fairfax Street
Alexandria, VA 22314
https://www.unitedway.org/get-involved/groups/student
The youth branch of United Way, Student United Way, works to help determine and alleviate community needs.

Volunteer Match
https://volunteermatch.org
Volunteer Match helps match volunteers to opportunities in their area of interest.

YMCA of the USA
101 N. Wacker Drive
Chicago, IL 60606
https://www.ymca.net/
Originally known as the Young Men's Christian Association, the Y is a worldwide organization dedicated to youth development, healthy living, and social responsibility. The Y offers teens opportunities to participate in community service programs.

Youth Activism Project
3909 Prospect Street
Kensington, MD 20895
https://youthactivismproject.org/
The Youth Activism Project helps teen activists build the skills, networks, and resources to lead change in their community.

Youth Service America
1050 Connecticut Avenue NW, #65525
Washington, DC 20035
https://ysa.org/
Youth Service America (YSA) helps youth and their adult mentors plan high-quality, high-impact service and service-learning projects, and offers grants for youth-led service projects.

Youth Volunteer Corps
1025 Jefferson Street
Kansas City, MO 64105
https://www.yvc.org/about-us/
Youth Volunteer Corps (YVC) is a network of affiliated organizations engaging youth in team-based, structured, diverse, flexible service-learning opportunities.

BIBLIOGRAPHY

Boal, John R. et al. *Chicken Soup for the Volunteer's Soul: Stories to Celebrate the Spirit of Courage, Caring, and Community.* New York: Simon and Schuster, 2001.

Brain, Marshall. *The Teenager's Guide to the Real World.* Raleigh, NC: BYG Publishing, 1997.

Clinton, Chelsea. *It's Your World: Get Informed, Get Inspired, and Get Going!* New York: Puffin, 2017.

Gay, Kathlyn. *Volunteering: The Ultimate Teen Guide.* It Happened to Me, no. 9. Lanham, MD: Scarecrow, 2007.

Joos, Kristin E., and Alana Rush. *Don't Just Count Your Hours, Make Your Hours Count: The Essential Guide to Volunteering and Community Service.* Lakeland, FL: TreeTop Software Company, 2010.

Lewis, Barbara A. *The Kid's Guide to Service Projects: Over 500 Service Ideas for Young People Who Want to Make a Difference,* 2nd ed. Minneapolis, MN: Free Spirit Publishing, 2009.

Perry, Susan K. *Catch the Spirit: Teen Volunteers Tell How They Make a Difference.* Danbury, CT: Franklin Watts, 2000.

Rosenberg, Bob, with Guy Lampard. *Giving from Your Heart: A Guide to Volunteering.* Lincoln, NE: iUniverse, 2005.

INDEX

Note: Page references for figures are italicized.

ABOUT THE AUTHOR

Jean Rawitt began her volunteer service as a fifteen-year-old candy striper at her local hospital. Years later, following careers as an executive in book publishing, marketing, public relations, and fundraising, she returned to volunteer service at Mount Sinai Hospital in New York City, where she went on to develop, coordinate, and supervise a number of volunteer programs, one of which was Mount Sinai Hospital's Varsity Volunteer Corps, a volunteer program for high school students.